Lone Star Quilts
and Beyond

Step-by-Step
Projects and
Inspiration

Jan P. Krentz

Think Stars!

Jan P. Krentz

C&T PUBLISHING

Copyright 2001 by Jan P. Krentz

Editor: Jan Grigsby
Technical Editor: Peggy Strawhorn Kass
Copy Editor: Lucy Grijalva
Design Director/Book Designer: Aliza Shalit
Cover Design & Production: Aliza Shalit
Production Assistant: Tim Manibusan
Graphic Illustrations: Kirstie L. McCormick
Front Cover Image *Summer Salsa*, Jan P. Krentz
Back Cover Image: *First Nectar*, Patricia Votruba
Quilt Photography: Carina Woolrich
How-to Photography: Bagley Tauber Photography
How-to Photography on page 51: Steven Buckley,
Photographic Reflections

Attention Teachers:

C&T Publishing, Inc. encourages you to use this book as a text for teaching. Contact us at 800-284-1114 or www.ctpub.com for more information about the C&T Teachers Program.

Library of Congress Cataloging-in-Publication Data
Krentz, Jan P.,
   Lone star quilts and beyond : step-by-step projects and inspiration / Jan P. Krentz.
      p. cm.
Includes bibliographical references and index.
   ISBN 1-57120-161-0 (paper trade)
   1. Patchwork—Patterns. 2. Star quilts—Design. I. Title.
   TT835 .K76 2001
   746.46'041—dc21

                  2001002432

Published by C&T Publishing, Inc.
P.O. Box 1456
Lafayette, California 94549

Printed in China
10   9   8   7   6   5   4   3   2   1

dedication

With love to my parents, Ray and Joie Poulsen who instilled in me the love of God, family, and country.
In memory of my father, H. Ray Poulsen, Jr. 1932 – 2000
Love to Don, Ryan, Dan, and Lindsay — you are my life!

CONTENTS

Acknowledgments

none of us is an island – we are each a colorful composite of a lifetime of relationships, experiences, education, and observation of the world around us. I wish to thank all those who have shaped me until now.

Praise God, who had a divine plan from the beginning! Continual thanks to my parents, Ray and Joie Poulsen, who trained me in "the way that I should go." Visiting my parents at the end of Dad's illness, I typed at his computer while he answered mail. This dear memory will forever remain when I think of this book and Dad.

My mother shared the joy of sewing with us from our childhood and my maternal grandmother, Bernice Madelon George, embodied the very essence of an independent, high-spirited woman. My husband's parents, Betty and Gordon Krentz, have been the most loving second family one could ask for.

Special recognition and praise go to my husband Don, and our children, Ryan, Dan, and Lindsay, who tolerated much during the work on this project, filling in the gaps at home.

My humble thanks to the many professional quilting teachers who challenged me to pursue skills and goals beyond my reach, and gratitude to loyal quilting students for their eager desire to learn.

Life is an ever-changing, living flow – people exchanging love, knowledge, kindness, and support from one to the next. I humbly thank the women who have shared their work in this book: Betty Alofs, Kathy Butler, Susan Cleveland, Jessie Harrison, Pam Kay, Suzanne Kistler, Lynne Lichtenstern, Alison Morton, Charlotte Rogers, Patricia Votruba, and Kathy Veltkamp. Their quilts grace these pages, allowing you to share in the fun we have had making star quilts. Sincere thanks to treasured friends: Bobbi Moore, Carol Pouliot, Betty Alofs and Lynne Lichtenstern for their mentoring, editing, encouragement, and technical expertise.

Sincere thanks goes to the talented C & T staff – Jan, Peggy, Aliza, Kirstie, Lucy, Stacy, and Tim – whose artistry brought the book to life. Special recognition goes to Carina Woolrich and Bagley Tauber Studio for their excellent photographs.

Thanks to:
* Tuesday Night Quilting Bee (San Diego, CA)
* Common Threads Quilt Guild (Lemoore, CA)
* Friendship Quilters (Poway, CA)
* Valley Oak Quilters (Tulare, CA)
* Quilter's Unlimited (Fairfax, VA)
* Monterey Peninsula Quilt Guild (Pacific Grove, CA)
* Empty Spools Seminars (Asilomar, Pacific Grove, CA)
* C&T Teacher Development Seminars

I am excited to see the new innovative quilts and share ideas with people in the future. Hopefully, we will cross paths one day. Thank you for "playing Lone Star!"

Jan P. Krentz

Introduction

Lone Star Quilts and Beyond: Step-by Step Projects and Inspiration presents a contemporary, artistic approach to one of America's most beloved quilt designs. It does not retrace the design's historic origins, but takes quilters to the next realm of Lone Star quilts. Exciting block designs and diamond variations guarantee your next project will be a creative adventure!

Traditional Lone Star or Star of Bethlehem designs feature 45° diamonds, individually cut and pieced in diagonal rows or segments, then joined to form larger diamond units, and finally combined with setting squares to create the large quilt surface. Surrounding areas were designed with appliqué blocks, pieced borders, lavish quilting, and more. This design required great skill and patience, and displayed the quiltmaker's technical expertise.

Current quiltmaking techniques have simplified the construction of this challenging star design. Using the rotary cutter and strip-piecing methods, quiltmakers of all levels experience great success.

The Lone Star design is ideal as a central medallion, and is often sewn as a square composition. Additional diamond units surrounding the central star medallion may position the color bands extending from point to point, so the colors form a "halo" around the central star. To create a rectangular design, additional borders and elements are added to change the quilt's shape.

The following chapters include a variety of design suggestions and patterns to customize your next star quilt into an artistic show-stopper. Mix, match, and combine various components to create eye-catching, creative Lone Star designs. Using a simple "paste-up" technique, and viewing the segment in repeat with design mirrors, you will rapidly conquer fabric selection and placement.

I know you will find this quilt design process to be fun, addictive, challenging, satisfying, and inspirational! Visit the quilt photos in the gallery, and try several of the projects.

Lone Star Basics
LeMoyne Star, Lone Star, and Star of Bethlehem

many historic volumes have been written about this classic eight-pointed star, known as Lone Star, Star of Bethlehem, or Morning Star. This book presents a contemporary, artistic approach to one of America's most beloved quilt designs.

A single, eight-pointed star made of 45° diamonds is commonly called the LeMoyne Star. The traditional Lone Star or Star of Bethlehem is based upon rows of 45° diamonds, set with their tips aligned in the center. The contrasting fabrics create circular rings, radiating from the star's center to the tips. It is a powerfully graphic design.

Contemporary quilt artists have updated the appearance of traditional Lone Stars by altering the color placement in the central diamonds and adding various elements surrounding the central star.

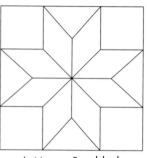 

LeMoyne Star block   Lone Star quilt design

Lone Star Quilt, circa 1930.
Maker unknown, 71" x 71"

DESIGN PRINCIPLES
Scale—Size of the Central Star and Finished Quilt

A star quilt's dimensions are determined by several factors:

* the number of diamond rows that create the star center
* the size and scale of the diamonds used
* the setting design surrounding the star.

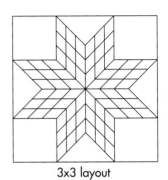

3x3 layout

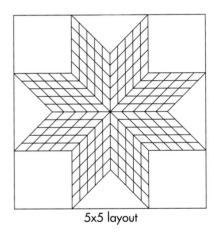

5x5 layout

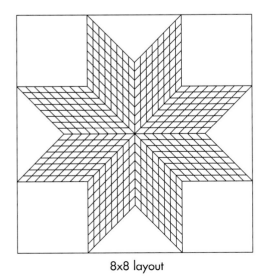

8x8 layout

Consider proportion and balance when designing your quilt. If planning a bed-sized quilt, for example, the scale of the central star medallion would need to be much larger than for a wall hanging or a garment.

You will determine whether your quilt needs a large central star with numerous rows of diamonds, or a smaller-scale star with fewer rows of diamonds. The projects and gallery may help provide inspiration for you when determining the finished size of your project.

Diamond Size—Strip Size

One way you can adjust the quilt's finished dimensions is by enlarging or reducing the size of the diamond. This is easily achieved when cutting strips with a rotary cutter. As diamond sizes are increased by ¼" increments, the overall measurement of the finished star is dramatically increased. A chart appears on page 110 to help figure the finished star sizes.

DESIGN TOOLS

Visualize a traditional Nine-Patch block with nine squares, arranged in three rows of three blocks per row. This is a 3 x 3 block arrangement. A unit with 9 diamonds, in three rows of three diamonds each, is called a 3 x 3 layout. Lone Star quilts may have as many rows of diamonds as you desire. Note the different layouts at the left.

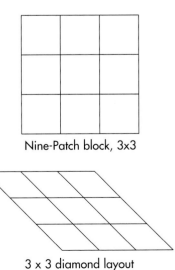

Nine-Patch block, 3x3

3 x 3 diamond layout

Design Paste-Up

A simple "design paste-up" guide will help you position colors in a pleasing arrangement for a basic Lone Star quilt. There are hundreds of options for arranging the fabrics, greatly affecting the finished star's appearance. Each project has a line drawing, showing the base layout of the design. Your fabric selection and surface embellishment will enhance these basic designs.

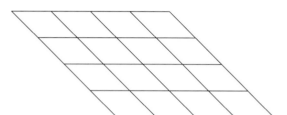

Paste-up for a simple 4 x 4 diamond unit

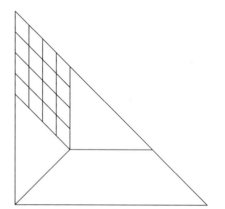

⅛ of quilt paste-up including setting pieces, use with design mirrors as a design tool

Completed design as illustrated in ⅛ quilt paste-up above

Design Mirrors

Preview the whole star design using a pair of hinged mirrors, with the hinge positioned at the narrow point of your design paste-up. Study the multiplied, reflected image. A dramatic change occurs as you move pieces, viewing each composition. Move the mirrors to the diamond's opposite tip, and view the design from this new perspective.

Design mirrors reflect the paste-up of the center star and possible borders.

Strip-Piecing Construction

When strip-piecing the Lone Star, you will sew several strips together. The strip placement determines the final pattern when the larger diamond segments are assembled. The paste-up is your pattern guide for positioning strips in the correct sequence.

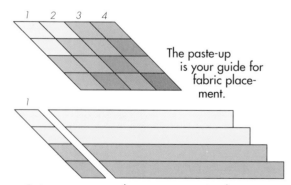

The paste-up is your guide for fabric placement.

Strip set corresponds to paste-up strip placement.

Adding Borders

Once the central design is complete, there are many options for creating borders for the Lone Star design. Traditionally, the central medallion is complemented by pieced or appliquéd blocks and borders, and finished with extensive quilting. Border designs increase the finished dimension of the quilt.

Chapter 3, Design Options and Paste-ups, provides a wealth of resources for designing your own Lone Star masterpiece! Play with a variety of corners, triangles, layouts, and borders in a smaller scale, and preview them with the design mirrors.

Selecting Fabrics

When sewing my own quilts, I prefer to work with a large number of fabrics. The variety of textures, tones, patterns, prints, and colors excites me! I never figure yardage for my own work, preferring to collect a stack of fabrics that I plan to sew together for a project. While studying the design, I assign different design areas to different color groups. Then, I use a group of similar fabrics interchangeably in the same position throughout the quilt. In Chapter 2 fabric selection is discussed more thoroughly.

Audition fabrics for center star and setting pieces using design mirrors.

2 Fabric Selection

Selecting the fabrics for your Lone Star quilt design is challenging and exhilarating! You'll be amazed at the visual patterns created by repeating fabrics in a symmetrical, radiating design. The star can be the central focal point, or serve as a subtle backdrop for appliqué. There are numerous methods for selecting fabric. Some quilters may work intuitively, while others follow a specific technique for color selection. The following fabric selection suggestions may enhance your color palette and create a successful, exciting quilt.

ESSENTIAL FABRIC PRINCIPLES – BASIC GUIDELINES

Contrast

Interesting quilts have pleasing contrasts between the fabrics used. Gather fabrics with light, medium, and dark values. Develop your ability to see value (lightness to darkness) rather than color.

Artists use terms such as tint and shade when referring to light and dark values of the same color. A tint is the color plus white (example: red plus white yields various values of pink). A shade is the color plus black (example: red plus black results in darker values of wine, burgundy, and reddish-black).

Scale

Select fabrics with a variety of printed or woven designs. Be sure to collect stripes, plaids, florals, tone-on-tone fabrics, and prints with large, medium and small motifs. The different fabrics create visual interest in your quilt, and are more fun to work with. The finished quilt is more beautiful and exciting with a variety of prints in the design.

Color

Select the overall color theme. For example, imagine you want to create a design that is predominantly blue. Select several delicious fabrics in a variety of blue shades. Now add a few coordinating colors, and a few small areas of bright contrasting colors (zingers) for refreshing accents. The predominant tone will be blue, but it will be much richer and more interesting with the added variety.

Contrasting Color Highlights

When preparing food, the chef seasons a dish with small amounts of herbs and spices. A small amount of colorful spice enhances without overpowering the dish, adding visual interest and savory contrast.

Creating contrast within your Lone Star is much like being a "fabric chef." You are "preparing" a great design, using fabrics and color in various amounts to create a luscious composition. A safe, predictable (perhaps boring) color palette is enhanced by adding small amounts of surprising contrast, color, or texture to the quilt design.

ADDING FABRIC ZINGERS

A "zinger" fabric can be almost anything—a surprising visual texture, pattern, or color that is unexpected, and used sparingly. Zingers add sparkle and interest to the design because they contrast the overall color palette of the design. It may be a complementary color (one which appears opposite on the color wheel), or a lighter or more intense shade of a color appearing in the star.

Study the following photos to see the difference a zinger fabric makes to the star.

Top: Red split diamond is a zinger;
Middle: Orange diamond is a zinger;
Bottom: Lime diamond is a zinger.

WORKING WITH PRE-PRINTED THEME FABRICS

For centuries, fabrics have been designed and printed in a myriad of lovely patterns; from florals, geometrics, stripes, plaids, and whimsical theme prints; to bold, contemporary, and abstract designs. There are patterns resembling pieced or appliquéd quilt designs, and scenes created for home decoration such as pillow tops and children's quilts. Using border prints and pillow panels offer great themes for building a Lone Star, as shown in some of the projects in this book.

USING FABRICS WITH UNIQUE FIBER CONTENT

Fabric choices today are abundant. Woven fabrics of 100% cotton are the favorites among quilters. Cotton fabric is durable, holds a crease when pressed, and handles with ease. Although 100% cotton fabric can be scorched when pressed by extremely high temperatures, it withstands steam and hot iron settings admirably.

Wall hangings or quilts designed exclusively for display are not subjected to the rigors of daily use. Consequently fabric choices may be much more varied for those quilts. Woven brocades, shimmering silks, metallic lamés, nubby raw silks or tweeds, sheer netting, tulle, and chiffon are all interesting choices to enhance your design.

If you select specialty fabrics with a variety of fiber contents for your designs, they can be challenging to use, requiring careful selection, and consideration of the following conditions:

※ Select fabrics of similar weight and thread count. A loosely woven fabric will unravel easily when sewn next to a durable, heavy-weight woven fabric. Stabilize loosely woven or fragile fabrics with a fusible, woven interfacing.

※ Lower iron temperatures if you are working with lamé or synthetic fabrics. Heat-sensitive fabrics may melt or shrink in size when touched briefly with a hot iron at cotton settings. Use a pressing cloth or appliqué pressing sheet to protect man-made specialty fabrics.

※ Colorful natural fibers will gradually fade over time, while synthetic fibers are frequently colorfast. Home decorator fabrics are treated with special sizing and fabric finishes, rendering them more colorfast than quilting or clothing fabrics. This factor may be critical when the natural cotton fabrics soften in color, and the occasional synthetic fabrics remain bright and bold in the design.

Sheer overlays may require special surface stitching or low-melt fusible adhesives to enhance their appearance. Unique threads such as thin Mylar®, ribbon floss, rayon, or perle cotton may require special machine needles, lower machine thread tension, and slower sewing speeds. Heavier-gauge decorative threads may be used in the bobbin. Stitching from the back of the project allows the bobbin thread to show on the top of the quilt.

Design Options & Paste-ups

3

DESIGN AREAS

Lone Star quilts have several areas available to add interesting, unique details.

"Center Stage" – Lone Star Medallion

The Center Stage

Broken Star Quilt, circa 1930.
Maker unknown, 68" x 73"

Traditionally, the star medallion is the "main attraction." Usually a central focal point, the star can also serve as a lovely backdrop for scenes or appliqué. In vintage Lone Star quilts, like the *Broken Star* shown at right, the concentric diamond bands form a powerful graphic image, demanding a symmetrical layout.

You'll discover many design possibilities when studying the symmetrical arrangement of diamonds. Variations could include but are not limited to any of the following:

* Unexpected fabrics
* Highlight and zinger colors
* Varying positions of fabrics from one diamond unit to the next
* Combinations of four diamonds to create double diamond units

* Special details and embellishments for interest

Make it Dynamic!

One of the most concentrated visual areas is the very center, where the eight diamonds meet. Be selective in your fabric choice for this central focal point. If you choose a fabric that is similar to the background, the star will appear to have a "hole" in the center. The effect could be charming in a design where transparency is desired, such as a celestial star, snowflake, zodiac chart, or wheel. The visual effect becomes lighter and lacy when the background color appears within the central medallion, almost giving the appearance of "cutwork" in cloth or fine china.

Great Visual Effects through Fabric Placement and Color Contrast

Circular bands of color

Radiating color placement

Checkerboard color placement

Accent diamonds

Fussy-Cutting

The star's center is an ideal location for a repeated motif, creating a strong secondary design. This can be achieved with selectively cut diamonds—commonly called "fussy-cutting"—that repeat the same motif.

Using the design mirrors, study the fabrics you selected. Move the mirrors around the surface, watching the repeated reflection. Isolate interesting motifs, moving the mirrors to see the image at different angles, viewing just a portion of an image. This changes the appearance from an isolated motif to an interesting larger shape.

Appliqué Saves a Dull Center

If your Lone Star lacks good visual impact in the center, it's a perfect opportunity to challenge yourself to a design variation. Consider adding appliqué in the center of your star using printed motifs or geometric shapes from the fabric. Cut smaller diamonds and overlap seam intersections. Appliqué the diamonds in place by hand or by machine, thereby adding color and contrast to your quilt. If there is an impossible intersection that simply would not match, minimize its appearance with some well-placed appliqué motifs or surface embellishment.

Appliquéd diamonds–*Dragonfly Pond*

Appliquéd center–detail, *Mardi Gras*

Spinning, Radiating, or Concentric Stripes

Striped fabric is fascinating in the center of a star! Depending on the way you position the ruler for the strip, you can control the direction of the stripe in the finished diamonds. This is especially important if you want a dynamic center without the bulk of pieced seams coming together in a single intersection, as with pieced diamonds.

Here are different visual effects achieved with striped fabrics—each optical effect is determined by the initial angle of the ruler, and the direction of the stripe in the finished diamond.

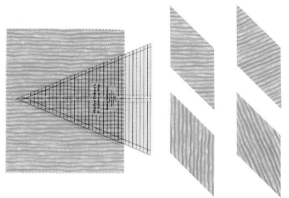
Changing the direction of the stripe creates different effects.

Stripes radiating from center point to outer tips

Stripes forming circles, side to side orientation

Stripes forming pinwheels

Stripes alternating direction in diamonds

Stripes forming chevrons

Designer Diamonds—Simple, Pieced, Appliquéd, and MORE!

Once you have explored and successfully pieced a Lone Star quilt, you will want to delve deeper into the world of the 45° diamond. There are thousands of ways to alter or enhance this basic shape!

Designer Diamond Options

Design sheets are on pages 22-25 for you to reproduce. Explore design ideas to change the surface of a single diamond. Remember—intricate designs within a single diamond may require increasing the scale of the piece. Study the design with the mirrors—see exciting patterns appear when simple diamond changes are repeated around the entire star.

Split diamonds from *Tea Time* page 76

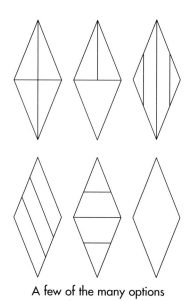

A few of the many options

Split diamonds from *Remembrance* page 84

Two-Color Split Diamonds

You can create two-color split diamonds by seaming two contrasting fabrics together. Press the seam allowance open. Orient the ruler so the seam runs vertically from tip to tip, or horizontally across the center of the diamond.

When pieced diamonds are located in the quilt center, you must contend with numerous seams (and bulk) meeting in the same intersection. Be patient, work carefully, and the final product will be worth the effort! Consider an angular position for the seam, creating a pinwheel effect in the center, and offsetting the bulky seams.

Split diamonds

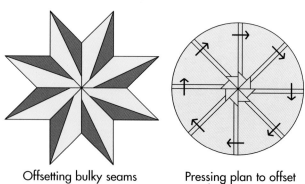

Offsetting bulky seams

Pressing plan to offset bulky seams.

"In the Wings" –
Setting Squares and Triangles

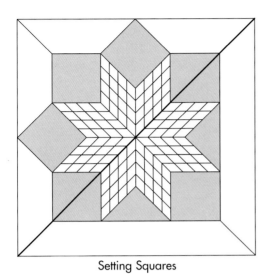

Setting Squares

The shapes surrounding the central star are very important. They complement the star, and enlarge the quilt's surface significantly. Traditional designs feature the star with four squares and four triangles, or eight setting squares.

Design options for setting pieces are numerous— select a light, solid color to display lovely hand quilting; feature appliqué, such as *Tea Time* (page 76), *Moon Dance* (page 30), *Crane Dance* (page 40), or *First Nectar* (page 42) quilts. Fussy-cut home decorator fabrics with bold flowers or geometric designs, complementing the star while coordinating it with the draperies or upholstery fabrics in the room.

Whether you are using eight squares, or a combination of squares and triangles, the designs surrounding the star should reflect similar elements while also complementing the star. Draw traditional pieced blocks to the specific scale required for your quilt. Diagonal block designs are particularly attractive. Page 24 features several block patterns; trace or copy the blocks, then cut out and glue them into a design paste-up. Use the design mirrors to evaluate various designs sur-

rounding the star. Mix and match "designer" diamonds, plain diamonds, and setting pieces for a truly individual quilt.

"The Supporting Cast"

Trapezoid Border Options

The choice for border design will be determined by the central theme of your quilt. Some quilts are calm and simple, requiring a complementary contrasting border. Antique Lone Star quilts were finished with a simple fabric strip border on all sides.

Trapezoid borders

For your quilt, draw a simple trapezoid border to fit around your setting blocks (see page 23).

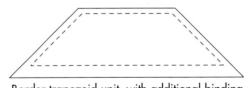

Border trapezoid unit, with additional binding space added at *outer edge*. Position the design elements inside the dotted lines.

Divide the trapezoid into geometric patterns or design appliqué that complements the center. This is the final prominent design area, and provides a stable visual edge to support the strong geometric star center. Evaluate several design sketches before you select a border pattern that truly enhances the quilt.

Simple strips in the border area provide a bold solution, creating the visual effect of a background frame with the star suspended in the foreground. Study the *Fiesta Star* (page 36) or *Flags & Fizz, Fun on the Fourth* (page 29) to see examples of this border style.

Secondary Diamond Units

Secondary diamond units

When a star medallion is set with eight squares, it is simple to add diamond units of the same dimension as the star center, forming an additional "halo" or "ring" of diamonds toward the outer border. Study the effect of these supporting cast members in *Summer Salsa* (page 100), *Double Cappuccino* (page 44), or *Blast Off* (page 45).

Two different border options

Blast Off

Summer Salsa

Spiral Lone Star

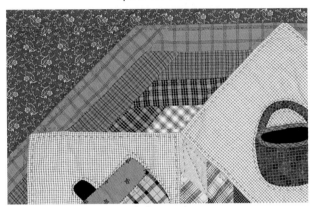

Bushel o' Baskets

To plan additional supporting diamond units, simply draw additional diamonds surrounding the eight setting squares. The strip dimensions—identical to the center star—are cut and sewn at the same time. Use the mirrored paste-up design to plan fabric and color placement in the secondary diamond units.

A charming variation of the pieced diamonds is a striped diamond unit, seen in *Spiral Lone Star* (page 92), *Undersea Reef* (page 43) or *Bushel o' Baskets* (page 33).

"The Grand Finale"

Once the quilt top is completed, you are ready for the final stages of finishing your quilt. Do not overlook the importance of lavish quilting patterns, surface designs provided by beading or couching, and decorative accents provided by additional items sewn to the quilt. Many of these items must be added following the quilting, and truly finish the quilt.

Undersea Reef

WORKSHEETS AND DESIGN INSPIRATION

Use the following pages to design a Lone Star variation. Trace, then mix-and-match segments to create your own original pattern.

You do not need to assemble the entire star. Simply cut and paste various units, and review the design with the hinged design mirrors. Use colored pencils to shade in areas, helping define the design. Be sure to include light, medium, and dark values in the design.

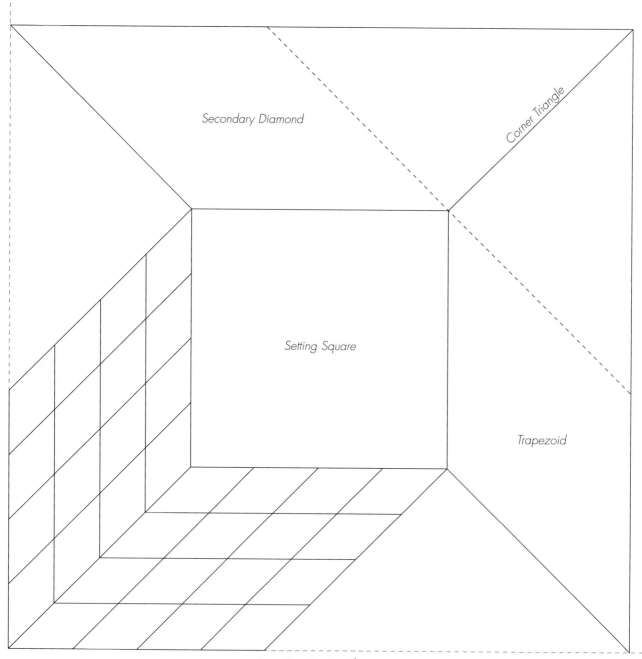

Lone Star Design Sheet
Paste design units in position. Evaluate with design mirrors.

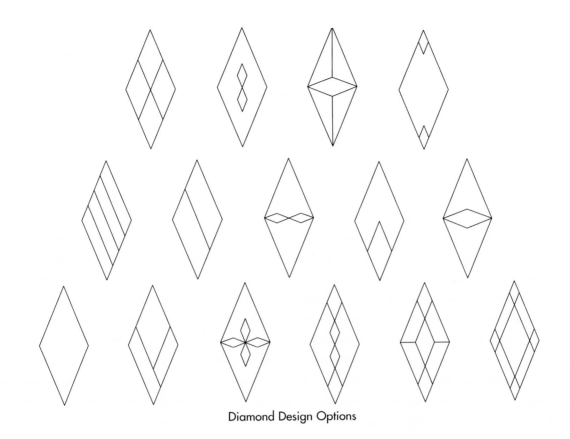

Diamond Design Options

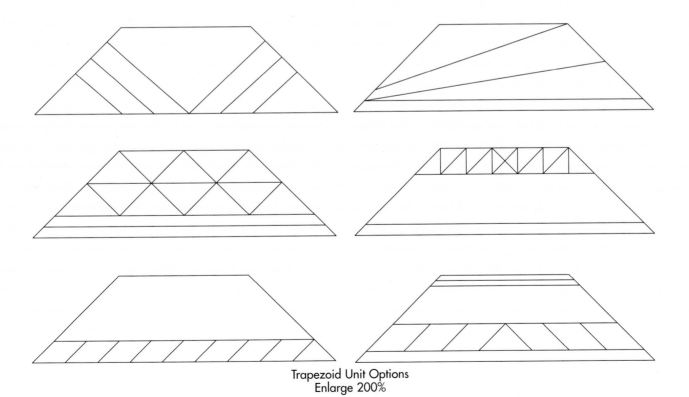

Trapezoid Unit Options
Enlarge 200%

Setting Square Design Options
Enlarge 200%

Corner Ideas
Enlarge 179%

PARTY OF THREE ✳ SUSAN CLEVELAND
2000. 56" x 45"

This quilt features precision piecing, thread work, and color! Susan used colorful, solid, hand-dyed fabrics, and several different threads; both through the needle and in the bobbin, to create this happy quilt. To add detail and accentuate the piecing, piping was added in the piecing and in the binding. Prairie points scattered in the binding add interest at the quilt's edge. Machine pieced and embellished, hand and machine quilted.

EVENING RADIANCE ✻ BETTY ALOFS
2000. 88" x 91"

Betty loves the color purple. She had collected fabrics for this quilt over time, and purchased the rest while taking a Radiant Star class in 1998. Machine pieced by Betty Alofs, machine quilted by Lori McManus.

CALIFORNIA LONESTAR ✳ ALISON MORTON

1998. 59" x 59"

Alison hand quilted this, her first Lone Star quilt, while traveling throughout the state of California. The hand quilting features numerous star patterns. Machine pieced and hand quilted.

FLAGS AND FIZZ ✳ SUZANNE KISTLER
Fun on the Fourth of July
47" x 47"

Uncomfortable with the challenge of working with diamonds, Suzanne selected a favorite fabric from her stash—the sunflowers and flag print—pulling the companion fabrics to match. She never realized the finished quilt would remind her of fireworks and the Fourth of July. This quilt became the first of many star quilts since Suzanne has caught "Lone Star fever." Machine pieced and hand quilted.

MOON DANCE ✳ PATRICIA VOTRUBA
2000. 44" x 44"

A simple lone star arrangement is enhanced with joyful appliqué designs of the sun and phases of the moon. Patricia used different background colors in the setting squares and extensive machine appliqué. The clouds feature sheer fabrics, allowing the images to peek through. Machine pieced, appliquéd, and quilted.

VIOLETS AND IVY ✳ JAN KRENTZ
1998. 54" x 54"

This quilt was made as a shop sample for a fabric store in Hanford, CA. The fabrics are home decorator glazed chintzes and 100% cotton prints. The star is strip pieced and the setting squares are fussy-cut from the large-scale print. Machine pieced and quilted.

GOOD THINGS GROW IN MY FRIEND'S GARDEN
2000. 48" x 48"
✳ SUZANNE KISTLER

Suzanne made this quilt as a gift for her friend, Elaine Short, who shares her bountiful garden harvest with others. One day Suzanne envisioned a vegetable quilt featuring Elaine's produce—and promptly went to the quilt shop to purchase "dirt" fabric. While she was away at the store, Elaine had generously delivered more vegetables to the Kistler home! Machine pieced and quilted.

BUSHEL O' BASKETS ✳ PAM KAY
2000. 50" x 50"

Pam combined three of her passions: Baskets, homespun plaid fabrics, and primitive stitching to create with this quilt that begs to be cuddled! Machine pieced and hand quilted. Basket patterns from *Home Sweet Home* by Joined at the Hip, Avis Shirer and Tammy Johnson.

FLAMING DIJON ✳ PAM KAY
2000. 45" x 45"

The Kay family has traveled to France, hosted a French exchange student, and sent their daughter to live as an exchange student in France. Pam loved creating this little "Ooh la la!" quilt using Provence fabrics! Machine pieced and quilted.

PEPPERMINTS IN TEA ✳ PATRICIA VOTRUBA

2000. 31" x 31"

Inspired by the author's *Tea Time* quilt (page 76), Patricia created a smaller-scale quilt, using eyelet lace, appliquéd pre-printed teacup motifs, and lively colors. The red-and-white split diamonds reminded Patricia of peppermint candies. Machine pieced, appliquéd, and quilted.

FIESTA LONE STAR ✳ CHARLOTTE ROGERS
1998. 42" x 42"

This is Charlotte's first Lone Star quilt. She was challenged to "think outside the box," and created two different sets of diamond units for the center. Her corner treatment is simple and effective. Machine pieced and quilted.

MARDI GRAS ✳ BETTY ALOFS
2000. 46" x 46"

Betty was challenged to use some wild and festive fabrics. The quilt is pieced, quilted, and surface embellished with a variety of beads, coins, and faux jewels. Mardi Gras masks and dimensional piecing add further detail. Machine pieced, appliquéd, quilted, and embellished.

WIMBLEDON STAR ✷ JESSIE HARRISON
1998. 24½" x 24½"

The colors of Wimbledon are purple and green—hence the name. The center diamonds are ½" in width. The corner stars are made of diamonds that measure ⅜" in width. The Wimbledon Star received the 2nd place award in the Traditional Pieced category, 1998 *Miniature Quilts Magazine* contest. Hand pieced and machine quilted.

PURPLE HAZE ✳ KATHY BUTLER
2000. 40" x 40"

This quilt has a shimmering surface. Kathy created the corner block patterns of her own design and intended the subtle colors to be compatible in an office or study. Machine pieced and quilted.

CRANE DANCE ✳ LYNNE LICHTENSTERN
2000. 46" x 46"

Lynne's inspiration always begins with the fabrics. This quilt features split diamonds, as well as appliquéd cranes from the Asian fabrics. Machine quilting designs with gold threads were inspired by Japanese Sashiko patterns. Machine pieced and appliquéd by L. Lichtenstern. Machine quilted by Carolyn Reynolds.

DO YOU SEE SPOTS? ✳ SUZANNE KISTLER
2000. 47" x 47"

Pete Kistler, a dairy veterinarian, requested a quilt for the office. Suzanne used the vibrant colors and cow-spot fabric specifically for viewing against the dark woodwork from twenty-five feet. Machine pieced and hand quilted.

FIRST NECTAR ✳ PATRICIA VOTRUBA
2000. 41" x 41"

Patricia's glorious Lone Star quilt features luscious appliquéd leaves, vines, and hummingbirds in the setting squares. The entire surface is further enhanced with fine beadwork and beautiful quilting patterns. Machine pieced, appliquéd, and embellished by P. Votruba. Machine quilted by Lisa Taylor.

UNDERSEA REEF ✳ BETTY ALOFS
2000. 55" x 55"

Betty has a passion for oceanic plants and fish. This quilt features natural and fantasy fish, textural kelp, appliquéd shells, and embellishments. The lower part of the quilt is darker, representing the ocean floor in the shadowy depths. Machine pieced, appliquéd, quilted, and embellished.

DOUBLE CAPPUCCINO ✳ JAN KRENTZ
2000. 48" x 48"

This quilt is the same pattern as *Summer Salsa* (page 100), with color placement creating a different visual design. The center of the star almost has a snowflake quality to it. Machine quilted mugs and cups of coffee with spiraling steam cover the quilt's surface. Machine pieced by J. Krentz, C. Pouliot, and L. Lichtenstern. Machine quilted by Carolyn Reynolds.

BLAST OFF ✳ ALISON MORTON
2000. 48" x 48"

A *Summer Salsa* (page 100) variation, Alison pieced the central star and rocket blocks, without the intricate pieced corners. Machine pieced, quilted, and embellished.

BREAST OF FRIENDS ✳ KATHRYN VELTKAMP
2000. 44" x 44"

Using Northcott Monarch "Quilt for a Cure" fabrics, this quilt was used as a fund-raiser for Breast Cancer Research. Machine pieced, appliquéd, and quilted.

CARIBBEAN CALYPSO ✳ KATHY BUTLER
2000. 46" x 46"

Kathy's first Lone Star quilt is an exciting view of colorful fish, plant life, shells, and pebbles. Numerous collections of found items embellish the quilt's surface. Machine pieced, quilted, and embellished.

WINTER LILY ✦ PATRICIA VOTRUBA
2000. 42" x 42"

Responding to a challenge by friends, Patricia proved that she could work in blue if she really set her mind to it! Waterlilies and lily pads are appliquéd in the setting squares. Machine pieced, appliquéd, and beaded by P. Votruba. Machine quilted by Lisa Taylor.

SPINNING JEWELS ✳ PATRICIA VOTRUBA
42" x 42"

Inspired by fabrics that reminded Patricia of rubies, garnets, emeralds, and citrine, she created a Lone Star design with movement and sparkle. The setting squares feature paper-pieced compasses and machine appliquéd poppies in sparkly fabrics. Machine pieced, appliquéd, and beaded by P. Votruba. Machine quilted by Lisa Taylor.

this chapter includes specific cutting, construction, and measurement details for a basic Lone Star quilt design. All of the Lone Star designs share the same basic construction techniques. Each of the projects found in the next chapter have unique elements or techniques that enhance the featured star.

Rainbow Lone Star

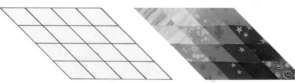

Rainbow Lone Star 4 x 4
line drawing and paste-up

When sewing the Lone Star, it is important to use a ¼" presser foot, or offset your machine needle so you are sewing an accurate scant ¼" seam. Seam lines must be very straight and consistent during the entire construction process. The finished star will fit together beautifully when precision, patience and accuracy are used each step of the way. Accuracy = Success!

✶ technique toolbox!

Tape a small acrylic ruler in front of your needle and presser foot. This provides a stiff edge to butt fabric against when guiding the strips under the needle.

This chapter explores a 4 x 4 design as shown on page 10. The fabric chart, paste-up design sheet, and yardage requirements are a guide. You will determine where the fabrics are placed as you design your quilt.

BASIC SUPPLIES AND EQUIPMENT

✶ Fabric: 100% cotton (easiest to work with) or cotton-polyester blends (more difficult)

✶ Rotary cutting equipment: rotary cutter with sharp blade, self-healing mat, acrylic cutting rulers of various sizes; large square, 6" x 24", 45° kaleidoscope ruler, or diamond specialty ruler, small square 2½"

✶ Sewing machine with ¼" presser foot for accurate seams

✶ Size 11-12 (70 or 80 Schmetz®) sewing machine needles for regular-weight cottons, 14-16 (90 or 100 Schmetz) for heavyweight fabrics

* Scissors, thread snips, seam ripper

* Design Mirrors: simple to make—**see below

* Fabric glue stick

* Sewing thread in medium shade to match fabrics

* Extra fine 0.5 shaft glass-headed pins for precision piecing and pressing

* ½ yard muslin or light-colored 100% cotton fabric for blocking cloth

* Spray starch or fabric finish

* Iron, ironing board, iron cleaner

* 1" x 2" mini self-stick notes

* Fusible web or bonding agent—select a stitchable product—one that will not "gum up" the needle with sticky residue when sewn

* Freezer paper and/or template plastic

* Optional—specialty fabrics: lamé, metallics, brocades, satins, laces, ribbons, sheer chiffon, silks, home decorator fabrics

* Optional—clear acrylic extension table for your sewing machine, VERY handy; also doubles as a light table when using a small fluorescent light underneath (for tracing patterns)

* Optional—2 yards, 72" wide white craft felt or flannel for design wall

** Have your local plastics store cut two 9" x 12" acrylic mirrors and tape one short side with duct tape to hinge them together.

WORKING WITH THE DESIGN PASTE-UP AND FABRIC PLACEMENT

* Copy the paste-up sheet.

* Select fabrics.

* Cut fabric pieces. Position them on the paste-up.

* Position the design mirrors on the paste-up, aligning the hinge at the narrow tip. Study the reflected star, positioning and rearranging fabrics until you like your design. Turn the paper 180° and position the mirrors at the opposite tip to see that effect, too.

* Permanently adhere fabrics to the paste-up with glue stick or Roxanne's Glue Baste-it™.

CUTTING FABRIC FOR THE CENTRAL STAR

Each diamond on the design paste-up represents one strip of fabric. There are sixteen different diamonds in a 4 x 4 layout. Cut sixteen individual strips of fabric from selvage to selvage. You may have several strips of the same fabric, as determined by your design paste-up.

* Cut sixteen strips 2¼" wide, for this Rainbow Star quilt.

* Fold the paste-up, isolating each row, and laying the strips in the order they will be stitched. Begin assembling the strips row by row.

Strip set 1

Strip set 2

Fold paste-up to isolate the strips
for sewing strip sets.

Strip sets 3 and 4

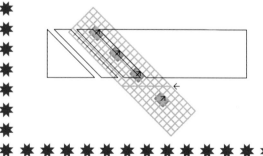
❋ Offset the ends of each strip one strip width, angling the strips in the same direction as the paste-up.

❋ Pin the strips together at the top edge to keep them in the proper order. Repeat for all four strip sets.

❋ Sew the groups of strips together as shown.

Making a Diamond Template

❋ With the regular acrylic ruler, draw two parallel lines on translucent template plastic, the same width as your cut strips.

❋ Turn the ruler, aligning the 45° guide with one of the parallel lines. Draw two parallel lines the same width as your cut strips. Draw the ¼" seam allowance INSIDE this diamond.

❋ Cut out the plastic template using a rotary cutter and ruler.

❋ Position the diamond template on the fabric, and trace the prominent design motifs on the template.

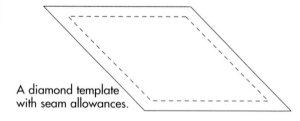

A diamond template
with seam allowances.

Using a Diamond Template for Fussy Cutting

❋ Position the template on your fabric, aligning the traced motifs on the template with the fabric images. Draw each of the eight diamonds on the fabric.

❋ Cut diamonds out on the lines using either the 45° kaleidoscope or regular acrylic ruler, and rotary cutter.

❋ When piecing the strip sets, the eight individual fussy-cut diamonds will be sewn to the adjacent strip. Allow approximately ½" space between each diamond as you sew them to the strip. Orient each diamond in the same direction, because it will affect the appearance if some of the diamonds are accidentally flipped. Add successive strips in the normal manner (see page 52). Press seams open, keeping strip sets straight.

✳ Lay the strip set on the cutting mat. Align the ruler with a pre-cut diamond, and align the 45° guide with a horizontal seam. Cut the eight strip units, allowing the individual diamond to determine ruler placement. There will be slivers of fabric trimmed away between the strips.

✳ Construction Tip:

Use only one row of individual diamonds when strip piecing a group of fabrics.

If your design calls for several pre-cut diamonds, separate the strip sets. Sew just one group of single diamonds to one or more successive strips. Press and cut. Sew partial strip sets together, forming the long continuous group of diamonds.

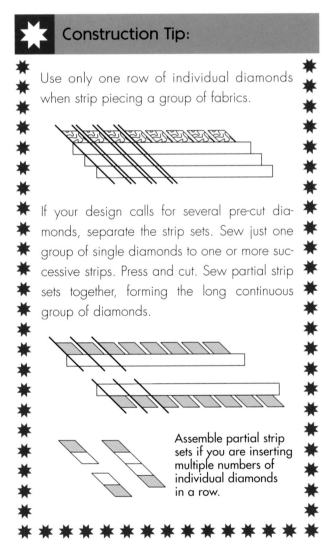

Assemble partial strip sets if you are inserting multiple numbers of individual diamonds in a row.

Making Split Diamonds

The following design method applies to all pre-pieced, split diamonds; whether horizontal, vertical, or diagonal. To determine the strip width:

1. Draw a diamond of the preferred finished size.

2. Draw the seam line where you want it to appear.

3. Measure the specific section with your ruler adding seam allowances, and cut a strip of contrasting fabric for each section measured.

4. Sew the fabrics together, and press the seams open.

5. Using an acrylic ruler and permanent ink pen, mark the underside of the 45° kaleidoscope ruler with the diamond size. (Ink can be removed with rubbing alcohol or an eraser.)

6. Mark the horizontal line, dividing the diamond in half widthwise. (You may also need to add the vertical line, dividing the diamond point to point, if the ruler is not pre-printed with this guideline.)

7. Cut the first two sides of the diamond, aligning the 45° kaleidoscope ruler over the pieced strips. The horizontal or vertical guideline will be aligned with the seam (depending on which type of diamond you are cutting).

8. Turn the ruler 180° and cut the remaining two sides.

9. Cut as many diamonds as your design requires.

10. Piece these individual diamonds into the strip sequence, as described in the Fussy Cutting section, page 16.

A Word About Fabric Grainline

One of the biggest difficulties encountered when sewing a Lone Star design is controlling and conquering the bias edges. Woven fabric has strong lengthwise (warp) threads and crosswise (weft) threads, creating stable structure in woven fabrics. The lengthwise grain, running parallel to the selvages, has no stretch or flexibility. The crosswise grain has slight stretch. The 45° diagonal line across woven fabric is the bias, which is stretchy and flexible.

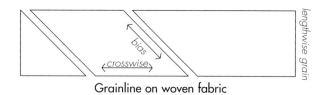

Grainline on woven fabric

Helpful tips when working with bias edges:

* Use spray starch when pressing the straight-grain strips before cutting them on the 45° diagonal. This adds crisp stability to the woven threads.

* Do not "stroke" the fabrics—this will cause stretching.

* Do not hold bias strips in the air or store them hanging from a hanger, clothesline, or drying rack causing gravity to stretch them.

* Resist the urge to over-handle the bias-cut strips.

* Do not iron or steam with great enthusiasm. "Attack ironing" causes the fibers to shift, stretch, and distort.

* Block the diamond units to set the grainline, as described on page 56.

Stabilize the Grainline

Spray the strip sets lightly with spray starch and press the seams open from the back. Keep the strip sets straight, with no curve, ruffle, or bend. Starch will help "set the grain" and control the bias once the strips are cut at a 45° angle.

 technique toolbox!

The diamond units may be positioned for right- or left-handed quilters by simply laying the strips right sides up or down. This allows you to cut on the correct side of the ruler.

STACK AND CUT STRIP SETS – MAKING THE 45° CUT

If the strips are straight, you may stack all four sets to cut the 45° angled strips simultaneously. If they are distorted in any way, you must cut the 45° strips individually for accuracy.

Stack strip sets in order, following the paste-up as a guide. You may cut the sets individually or stack them. If you stack them, then:

1. Place strip set #1 on the bottom.

2. Place strip set #2 on top, offsetting the upper edges by ½" as shown below, making sure the edges are parallel. Repeat for strip sets #3 and #4.

3. Place the acrylic ruler on the stacked strips. Slant the ruler until the 45° guideline is aligned with a horizontal raw edge or straight seam. The ruler should be angled in the same direction as the offset ends of the strip sets.

4. Make a "clean-up cut" at the end of the strips. Position the ruler, measuring the same width as the original strips (2¼" in this case) and begin cutting the 45° angled strips. Continually align the 45° guide along a horizontal seam or edge, and measure from the freshly cut end. You may need to make more than one clean-up cut. Cut eight sets total.

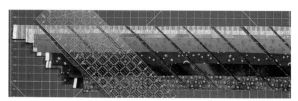

Cutting strip sets

SEWING DIAMOND STRIP SETS INTO UNITS

Lay out the four diamond strip sets in the same arrangement as your paste-up. Pay attention! It is very easy to lay the strips in opposite order, creating a different design! If you should accidentally sew the eight units with a different order, it is not a disaster! I recommend keeping the new design, because ripping the bias seams causes stretching and distortion.

Diamond strips sewn in reverse order

Diamond strips sewn in the correct order

PINNING FOR ACCURACY— POSITIONING PIN TECHNIQUE

Angled seams do not align in the same way as 90° intersections (as when sewing two squares together). Select a waste scrap from the cleanup cut, and snip out a small section that contains the seam and two fabrics. Cut a ½" to 1" piece. This will be your personal seam allowance gauge.

A small scrap becomes your personal seam allowance gauge.

1. Select two strip sets that will be sewn together. Place right sides together, and offset the two strips until you see a small ¼" triangle peeking out at the beginning of the seam line. You will always have a ¼" tip at both ends of every seam.

Use positioning pin to match seams, allowing a ¼" tip to extend at both ends of the seam line.

2. Holding the fabric seam gauge next to the first intersection, insert a pin through the seam allowance. Separate the two strips, inserting the pin tip through the second strip, piercing the seam. Keep the pin upright. Use two additional pins to hold the seams in place, inserting them perpendicular to the seam line on either side of the positioning pin. Pin all intersections, allowing a ¼" tip to overlap at both ends. Remove the positioning pin.

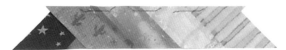

Baste 3-5 stitches at each intersection

3. Machine baste the intersections by sewing just 3-5 medium length stitches across an intersection; lift the presser foot, travel to the next intersection, sew 3-5 stitches, and so on. Remove the unit from the sewing machine, and open the two pieces. Check each intersection for a perfect match. If you need to re-align any of the sections and sew again, you have only a few stitches to undo and try again. Once satisfied, stitch the seam with a short stitch length (12-15 per inch, or 1.5-2 on metric machines). Sew all seams, creating eight diamond units.

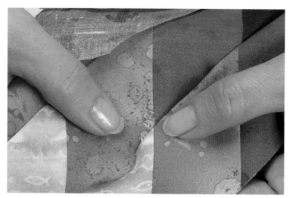

Check for a good seam alignment.

Sewing the unit

Sew all seams creating one leg of the star.

CREATING AND USING A BLOCKING CLOTH

1. Measure the finished size of several of the interior diamonds, then take the average width of these measurements.

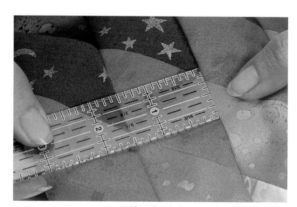

Measuring finished diamonds

2. Use a ½ yard piece of 100% cotton muslin or light-colored solid. Fabric blends are unsuitable for the blocking cloth, due to shrinkage and distortion.

3. With a permanent pen and acrylic ruler, draw a baseline about 18" long, parallel to the fabric edge.

4. Align the 45° guide with the baseline and draw the first line as shown below.

Baseline.

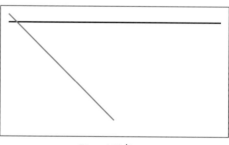

First 45° line.

5. Align the 45° guide on the baseline, and draw a second line the width of the average finished diamond measurement, intersecting the first line, and extending out on the muslin. Repeat, drawing a total of five lines.

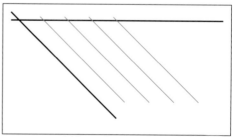

Add lines for your layout

6. Create four rows by drawing four lines parallel to the base line as shown. Add ¼" seam allowance on all sides.

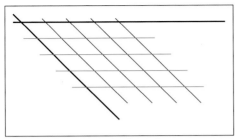

Drawing the lines for a
4x4 layout blocking cloth.

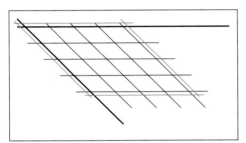

Adding ¼" seam allowances on all sides.

7. Place the blocking cloth on the ironing board. Position a pieced diamond unit, wrong side up, on top of the cloth. With glass-headed pins, begin pinning the diamond unit to the blocking cloth, aligning the seams with the guidelines. Work from the center to the tips on all four sides.

Pin the diamond unit to the blocking cloth

Pin the diamond unit in place,
working from the center to the corners.

8. Lightly mist the back of the unit with spray starch or water. Press the seams open from the back, blocking the unit to its finished shape. Allow the unit to cool. Repeat the blocking process for all eight diamond units.

Spray lightly with starch, and press seams open.
Allow to cool before removal.

MEASURING FOR SETTING SQUARES AND TRIANGLES

When the diamond units are complete, you will gauge all other sections of the quilt from their dimensions.

Align the raw edge with the ¼" mark on the ruler. Slide the ruler back from the raw edge just a fraction to allow for the dimension of the pencil or pen point. Mark all corners. Verify your accuracy by comparing the pencil line with the personal seam allowance snippet you saved from the cutting process.

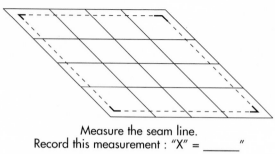

Measure the seam line.
Record this measurement : "X" = _____"

The seam line measurement is identified as "X." Setting squares, triangles, and trapezoid units all share measurement "X" as a seam line measurement.

Mark ¼" seams at all four corners of the diamond.

Diamond Units—Grainline

There are two types of grainline along the outer edges of the diamond units. The straight-grain side is very stable. The bias side is very stretchy. Measure first on the stable edge, from mark to mark at either end. Average several measurements, if necessary.

* To draw a setting triangle, draw a baseline on freezer paper or template plastic. Mark the measurement for seam line "X." Add a second side at right angles to the baseline, also "X" in length. Connect the two end points, forming a right triangle. Add seam allowance on all three sides of the setting triangle.

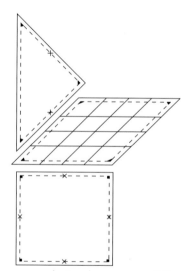

Setting squares and triangles measure "X" on the sides indicated.

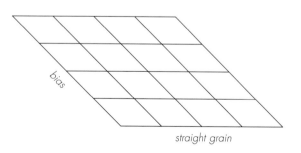

bias

straight grain

* To draw a setting square, draw a baseline on freezer paper or template plastic. Mark the dimension "X" on the line with two dots at either end. Draw a 90° line from each dot, creating sides 2 and 3 of the square; each of them also

measures "X" in length. Connect the sides with line 4, finishing the square. Add ¼" seam allowance around the outside of the square on all four sides.

Cut a paper or plastic template and use it to cut the fabric.

The Rainbow Lone Star design has four setting triangles and four squares. You may prefer to use eight setting squares instead. If you like, you might fussy-cut setting squares from decorative fabric, requiring additional yardage depending on the motif spacing.

SIMPLE TRAPEZOID BORDER

The wide outer border is simple to draw and construct. On freezer paper or template plastic, draw a baseline. Mark the "X" dimension dots toward the center of the line. Position the ruler, aligning the 45° guide along the baseline, and draw a line extending outward from both dots. Mark the "X" measurement on sides 2 and 3. Connect the dots, forming side 4 of the trapezoid shape. Add ¼" seam allowance on the first three sides, and add 1" on the longest side to allow extra fabric for trimming and binding.

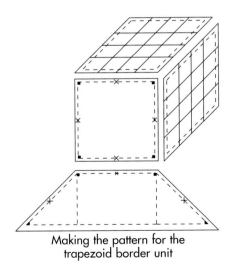

Making the pattern for the
trapezoid border unit

CONSTRUCTING THE LONE STAR WITH THE Y-SEAM TECHNIQUE

The "Y-Seam" method is taught by several of the nation's leading quilt instructors—Sharyn Craig, Ruth B. McDowell, Marsha McClosky, Sherry Reis, and others—with great success. This method allows assembly of the diamond units with more accurate results than the traditional process.

Read the complete assembly process before sewing. If you have never tried this method, please sew your Lone Star quilt top with this assembly method. The sewing order is slightly different from the traditional method, and will be described for Lone Stars using both setting squares and triangles, or eight setting squares, as featured in several of the projects in the next chapter.

PLEASE NOTE:
Test the seam width so you KNOW you're sewing a SCANT ¼" seam. The seam includes the line of thread plus the turn of the cloth after pressing. ALL of this must equal ¼".

1. Mark the tips and corners of all pieces with ¼" seams.

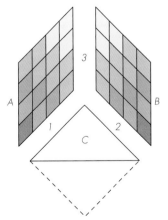

Layout for Y-seam construction
with sewing order

2. Lay the diamond units in two stacks by color, side by side (four diamond units per stack). The diamonds should mirror each other in color groupings.

3. Lay the setting triangles or squares C at the base of the two diamond stacks, filling in the opening between the diamond units.

4. Select one C triangle or square. Flip it right sides together toward an adjacent diamond unit A. Align seam lines, registering ¼" marks from the top piece to the diamond unit beneath it.

5. Sew the seam, stop and backstitch where indicated. Repeat for all four units, sewing the remaining diamond units to the adjacent setting pieces. FINGER-PRESS the seam away from the diamond unit on all four sets.

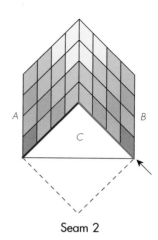

Seam 2

8. Flip two diamond units A and B right sides together, raw edges aligned. Piece C can fold inside the diamonds for easier sewing. Sew from the raw edges at the diamond tip toward the the setting square; stop and backstitch at the previous stitching.

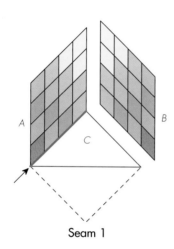

Seam 1

6. Return the sets to the original position alongside the remaining diamond units. Flip one A/C unit toward diamond B with right sides together. Align the two edges to be sewn, pinning seam to seam. With C on top, sew from seam to seam, stop, and backstitch. Repeat for remaining units.

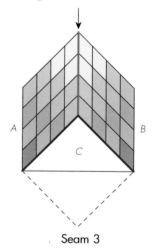

Seam 3

NOTE: When sewing up to the previous seam, it's OK to stop just short of the seam. If you sew too far, simply snip the single stitch crossing the previous seam line.

8. FINGER-PRESS the seams TOWARD C. Press the A/B seam toward B. Repeat for all components. You now have four diamond units with "Y" seams.

Four diamond units with Y-seams

Making the Quarter-Star Units

9. Flip one square D right sides together onto a diamond unit. Align raw edges and ¼" seam lines of both units. Sew D to the right edge of the diamond unit, stop and backstitch as before. Repeat for the remaining three units, creating four odd-shaped quarter-star units. Finger-press seam toward the setting piece D.

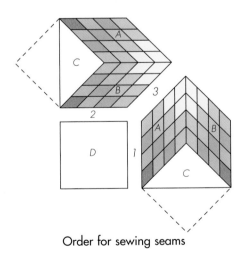

Order for sewing seams

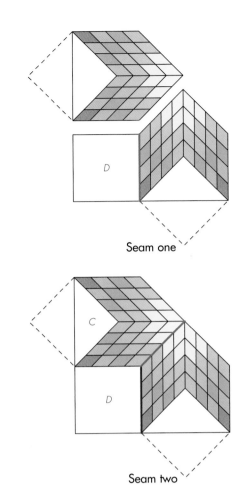

Seam one

Seam two

10. Position units for final assembly. The next seam will join D to the adjacent A. Flip one unit face down on the adjacent unit, keeping the seam aligned (the setting square will be on top, the diamond unit beneath it). Sew the seam line, backstitching as usual. Repeat with the remaining two pieces. Finger-press the seam allowances toward the squares.

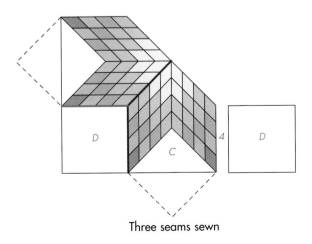

Three seams sewn

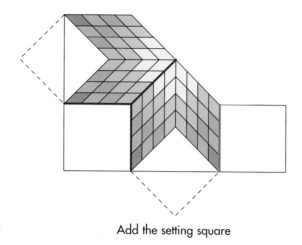

Add the setting square

11. Position the diamond pairs, right sides together, edges aligned. Sew from ¼" mark to mark, backstitching as usual. Repeat with remaining units. Finger-press, with seam allowances going the same direction as the previous diamond seams.

Sewing the Two Star Halves

12. Place the star halves right sides together and sew as shown.

Joining two halves at the center

Sewing the Center Star Seam

13. The last seam joins the star's center. Increase the stitch length on your sewing machine. Align the center seam intersections. (All seam allowances should alternate from previous finger-pressing.) Baste 3-5 stitches at the center intersection, open and check for good alignment. When satisfied, shorten the stitch length and sew the center seam, backstitching at both ends without crossing previous seams.

14. Add additional setting pieces (trapezoids, secondary diamonds) to the central star unit in a similar sequence as the Y-seam method you have just sewn. Seams are numbered for the piecing sequence, below. The final seams join corner triangles to the quilt top.

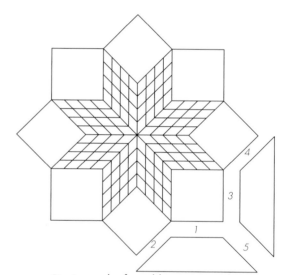

Piecing order for adding trapezoids

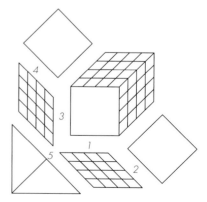

Piecing order when adding secondary diamonds and triangles

Professional Pressing Tip: A raised area with multiple seams will become glazed and shiny under the iron. Protect the raised fabric by using a pressing cloth when ironing.

Open the star quilt top. Flare the seam allowances on the back so that all seams rotate in the same direction. The long center seam will flip, changing direction at the center, resulting in a flat star center.

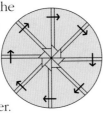

15. Press the quilt top without stretching. It should lie flat with a ¼" seam allowance at the outer edge of each star point.

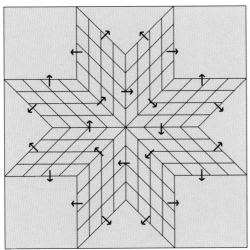

Seam allowances will rotate
around the center intersection

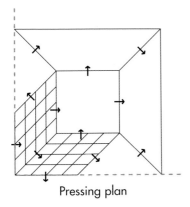

Pressing plan

projects

Safari

✴ jan krentz

2000. 64" x 64"

BEHIND THE SCENES

This striking Lone Star design features large pre-printed African animal pillow panels and coordinating animal fur prints. Although this theme is African, the basic design works well with any printed fabric collection. Select fabrics that are readily available to you.

Center Stage

The center star features two different fabrics for the first diamond strip. This creates an easy-to-piece two-color pinwheel in the center. Note the design created where four diamonds merge to make a double diamond unit. Fussy-cut a dynamic motif from a large-scale print fabric for this diamond.

The Supporting Cast

The central star medallion is surrounded by four corner squares and four setting triangles. The corners are pre-printed, and the triangles are pieced to replicate the same visual character that the corners provide. Since the pillow panels had borders of zebra and giraffe prints, the triangles also have borders from companion fabrics.

Detail of center star, *Safari*

The Grand Finale

The quilt has a strong, solid black border with exciting, free-motion stitching in metallic thread.

GETTING STARTED

Strip size: 3"
Finished star size (tip to tip): approximately 60"
Finished quilt size: approximately 66" x 66"
The layout is 5 x 5 with a double diamond.

A pre-printed pillow panel

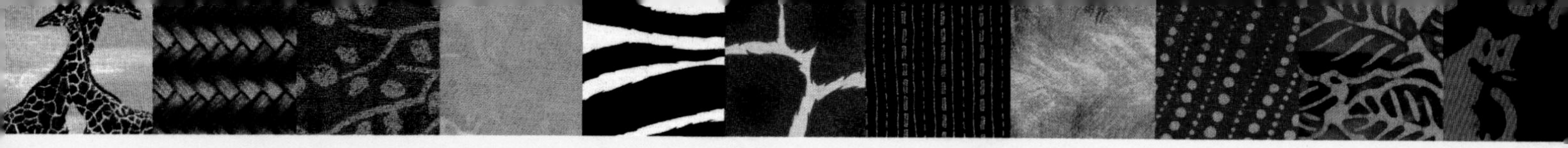

FABRIC REQUIREMENTS

FABRIC	AMOUNT	CUT
1 African Animal print	3 yards	5 - 3" strips (cut one in half) 8 - double diamonds 4 - setting triangles (cut later)
2 Rust colored batik	¼ yard	2 - 3" strips
3 Medium olive green print	⅜ yard	3 - 3" strips
4 Black/brown stripe	¼ yard	2 - 3" strips
5 Brown/tan stripe	½ yard	5 - 3" strips
6 Brown/black/rust print	¼ yard	2 - 3" strips
7 Zebra print	⅝ yard	3 - 3" strips 3 - 3½" strips (cut later)
8 Giraffe print	½ yard	4 - 3" strips 3 - 3½" strips (cut later)
9 Black w/brown cats batik	⅛ yard	1 - 3" strips
10 White w/small black dot	¼ yard	3 - 3" strips
11 Black solid	1 yard	7 - 3½" strips
12 African animals	18" pillow panels	2 - 2 pairs–do not cut apart (Note: the size of the pillow panels determines the size of the star diamonds)
100% Cotton muslin	⅜ yard	18" x 32" rectangle for blocking cloth

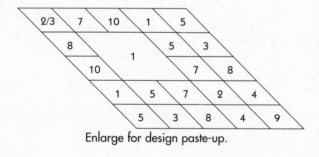

Enlarge for design paste-up.

MAKING THE STAR
Cutting Double Diamonds

This is a terrific Lone Star technique – easy and visually effective. Simply combine the size of a group of four diamonds – for instance, four 3" diamonds when sewn together measure 5½" x 5½" (remember to subtract center seam allowances between the four diamonds). Make a template to fussy-cut the fabric motif. Mark the ruler or template with the printed motif and cut eight identical diamond units.

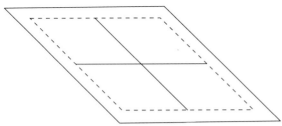

A double diamond is the same as a 2 x 2 unit.

1. Make a 5½" x 5½" template for the double diamond, see page 52.

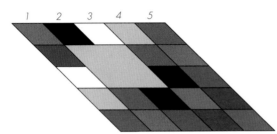

Combine four diamonds
to create a double diamond.

2. Follow the same basic plan for cutting and piecing strips together as discussed in Chapter Four, using two different fabrics for the first diamond in row 1 (see page 69). Cut 4 strips of row 1 with fabric 2, and 4 strips of row 1 with fabric 3 as the first diamond.

Note the short groups that fill in the rows on both ends of the double diamond unit (rows 2 and 3).

3. Offset the piecing of that strip set in the opposite direction from the other sets.

Strip set is staggered in the
opposite direction for reverse cut.

4. Cut the 45° angle as shown above. Cut eight.

5. Cut the remaining strip sets as usual, laying out the double diamond units following the design paste-up.

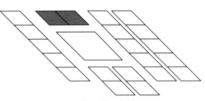

Note the shaded pair.
A reverse cut is required to make pieces fit.

6. Pin and sew the short rows surrounding the double diamond section first.

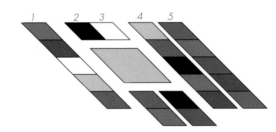

7. Sew these short rows to the double diamond, following the paste-up.

8. Sew the remaining rows of diamonds, forming 5 x 5 units. Block the units, pressing seams open.

ADDING THE SETTING SQUARES AND TRIANGLES

1. Measure the seam line of the diamond units for the star, as described on page 58. This dimension–"X" –becomes the side measurement for the setting squares and triangles. Draw patterns for these templates, adding ¼" seams on all sides. ("X" will be approximately 17½" for this quilt. It is important to find YOUR "X" measurement as it depends on YOUR seam allowances.)

2. Cut the pre-printed pillow panels to the correct size, using your "X" measurement (approximately 17½"). For smaller motifs, you may need to increase the pre-printed block size by adding additional borders.

3. Make a setting triangle template. Measure the border width from the printed pillow panel, and draw that width on the two short sides of the setting triangle. Draw a mitered seam where the two borders meet.

4. Working from this master pattern, trace individual pattern pieces for the smaller areas, adding ¼" seam allowance surrounding each piece. Keep the original draft for reference. Cut border strips. Cut four right triangles, positioning the longest side on the straight grain.

5. Apply the border to the setting triangle and miter the outside corner. Press.

6. Assemble the quilt top following Y-seam construction in Chapter 4.

ADDING THE FINISHING TOUCHES

1. Cut seven 3½" x 42" border strips. Sew the strips together to make four border strips. Apply the borders to the finished quilt top, miter corners, and trim the excess.

2. Create interesting quilting designs to enhance your quilt theme.

Safari border.
Quilting by Lisa Taylor.

The setting triangles complement the pre-printed setting squares.

Safari quilt layout

Dragonfly Pond

✳ jan krentz

2000. 46" x 46"

BEHIND THE SCENES

This quilt reminds me of a warm summer day with a breeze softly rustling the leaves, birds chirping, insects humming, and neighborhood children giggling nearby. The heavy scent of flowers in the air makes me feel lazy, carefree, and ready for a cool glass of lemonade.

Dragonfly Pond features some interesting additions to the basic Lone Star pattern. The color palette was inspired by the border print fabric used around the outer edge. The summer theme of grasses, blue sky, rich earth, and lightning bugs is enhanced by several different "bug" fabrics and various appliquéd dragonflies on the quilt's surface.

Center Stage

The center star features a collection of coordinating fabrics, fussy-cut center diamonds, and appliquéd accent diamonds.

The Supporting Cast

The surrounding setting squares are cut strategically from the border print. A cutting diagram is shown below. Note the four setting squares which are "on point," their outer corners reaching the bound edge. They are cut with the printed border crossing one tip so the visual shading is continuous from outside corners through the center of the star.

In the Wings

A second set of diamond units surrounds the central medallion, with colors running lengthwise through the unit, from tip to tip. Simple mitered corners display the entire border print.

The Grand Finale

The surface is quilted with a delightful, easy pattern of breezy grasses, swirls, and curls. I added a few appliquéd dragonflies, beaded dragonflies, lightning bugs, and flower stamens to the quilt's center.

GETTING STARTED

Strip size: 2¼"
Finished star size (tip to tip): approximately 33½"
Finished quilt size: approximately 46" x 46"
The layout is 4 x 4

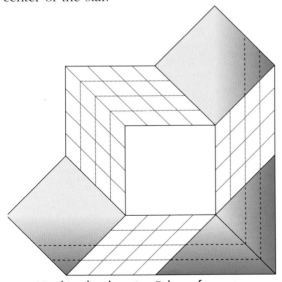

Matching border print. Enlarge for paste-up.

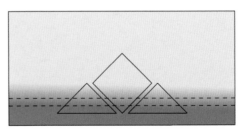

Layout on fabric matching border patterns on all pieces.

FABRIC REQUIREMENTS

FABRIC	AMOUNT	CUT
1 Lt. background, bug print	¼ yard	3 - 2¼" strips
2 Lt. med. Green	¼ yard	2 - 2¼" strips
3 Lt. background, dragonfly print	¼ yard	2 - 2¼" strips
4 Bright lt.-med. Peach	⅛ yard	1 - 2¼" strip
5 Med. green print	⅓ yard	4 - 2¼" strips
6 Dk. navy print	½ yard	5 - 2¼" strips
7 Lt. blue print	⅛ yard	1 - 2¼" strips
8 Med. smoky blue	⅓ yard	4 - 2¼" strips
9 Med. royal blue	½ yard	5 - 2¼" strips 1 - 1" strip*
10 Lt. background, floral print	¼ yard	2 - 2¼" strips
11 Rusty brown (color that coordinates with border print)	⅛ yard	1 - 2¼" strips
12 Med.-dk. lime green	¼ yard	2 - 2¼" strips
13 Bright Med.-dk. peach	⅛ yard	1 - 1" strip*
14 Border print yardage	At least 17 linear feet of border design, whether printed on one selvage or on both selvages.	8 - Setting triangles (cut later) 8 - Setting squares (cut later)
100% cotton muslin-blocking cloth	½ yard	18" x 22" - Cut later
Paper backed fusible web	⅓ yard	

* Optional appliqué diamonds

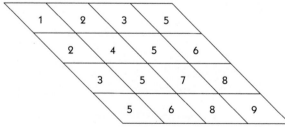

Star Diamond. Enlarge for paste-up.

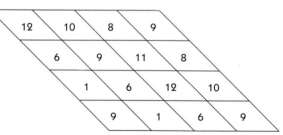

Secondary Diamond. Enlarge for paste-up.

MAKING THE STAR

1. Complete the paste-up and study the repeated image with design mirrors to evaluate fabric placement before cutting your strips.

2. Determine whether any of the fabrics would look best if fussy-cut. If so, following the guidelines on page 16, prepare a template and cut as many individual diamonds as your layout requires. In my quilt, the center diamonds were fussy-cut featuring two different printed dragonfly motifs.

3. Count each diamond of the same fabric. Keep a checklist, then add up the total. You should have 32 diamonds requiring 32 strips.

> Remember that each diamond on the paste-up represents one entire strip of fabric. Your quilt may require a combination of strips and fussy-cut diamonds.

4. You need to cut a total of 16 strips for the star diamonds AND 16 strips for the secondary diamonds.

5. Sew the strips in rows, offsetting the strips at an angle following your design paste-up. Press seams open.

6. Cut the strips at a 45° angle creating diamond rows.

7. Sew all 16 diamond units (eight for the central star and eight for the secondary diamonds). Create a blocking cloth. Block the units and press the seams open.

Setting square *Dragonfly Pond*

 technique toolbox!

TIPS FOR WORKING WITH LARGE PRINTS IN A SMALL DESIGN MOCK-UP

There are several methods for using a large-scale or border print to get the true appearance in a miniature paste-up:

* Use small slivers of the large-scale or border print in the outer corners and setting squares, collecting the prominent colors and sticking them down in roughly the right strata. Although it isn't exact, you get a sense of the color proportion compared to the pieced diamond units.

* Snap a photo or digital image of the large-scale or border print. Cut the finished photograph and glue it in place on your paste-up.

* Lay a piece of the large-scale or border print on the bed of a color copy machine. Reduce the image to the smallest percentage. Cut and paste the "printed fabric" in place.

ADDING THE SETTING SQUARES, TRIANGLES, AND TRAPEZOIDS

1. Measure the outer edges of several diamond units, take an average, and record this measurement: "X" = _____" (approximately 9¾", but be sure to use your own measurements).

2. Draw a square on freezer paper, using "X" as the side measurement. Add ¼" seam allowance on all sides.

3. Draw a corner triangle pattern, using "X" as the measurement for the short sides. Add ¼" seam allowance on the short sides.

4. Assemble the quilt top following Y-seam construction instructions in Chapter 4.

ADDING THE FINISHING TOUCHES

Study the quilt from a distance. Are there any areas that seem dull, or need a boost of color? If so, cut a few smaller scale diamonds in a contrasting color and position them on top of an intersection—between two or more diamonds. As you study the new additions, ask a friend or family member to remove them. Do you miss them? This now-you-see-it, now-you-don't approach is an effective way to audition design changes. Consider cutting a few medium-to-large scale print motifs, scatter them or cluster them, and evaluate the effect. Appliqué the diamonds to the quilt top as desired.

Quilting by Carolyn Reynolds

Create free-motion quilting designs that support your quilt's theme. The grasses, flowers, swirls, bugs, and clouds on *Dragonfly Pond* were beautifully quilted by Carolyn Reynolds, with 30-weight variegated thread.

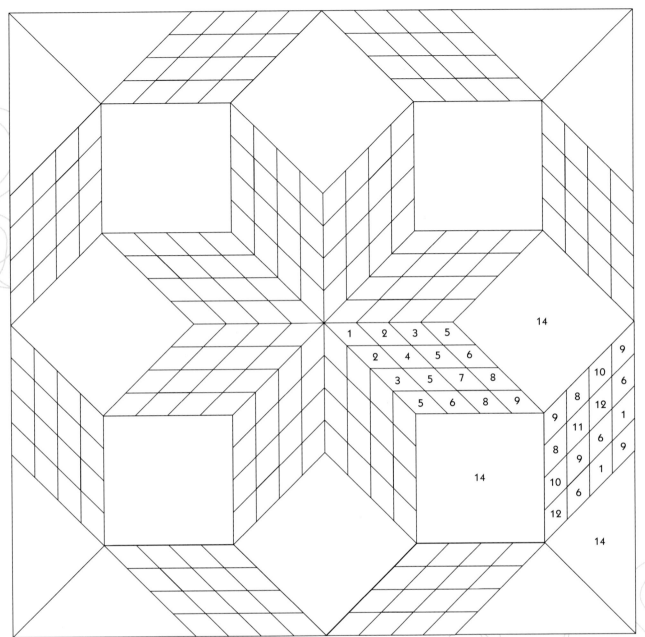

Dragonfly Pond quilt layout

Tea Time

jan krentz

2000. 47" x 47"

BEHIND THE SCENES

Get out the good china, and set a pretty table! It's *Tea Time*, a delightful Lone Star design with appliquéd teapots sitting primly on doilies surrounded by a double tablecloth border. The quilt evokes fond memories of entertaining friends in Grandma's parlor. Use the basic design and incorporate your favorite fabrics. Each lovely teapot can spotlight a gorgeous fabric from your collection.

Center Stage

The heart of this star features split "designer diamonds" with appliquéd accent diamonds that provide visual interest.

Supporting Cast

The setting squares are special. Note the fluted appliqué pieces that surround the star points. These soften the star's graphic appearance. The appliquéd lace doilies and teapots provide a cheerful and inviting element.

Split diamond center

A setting square.
Each teapot can be a special fabric.

In The Wings

The surrounding border is a double layer—an over-layer and an underskirt—that frames the central design and finishes the theme of afternoon tea. Select treasured family linens, border print fabrics, or embroidered window valances and use the embellished edges or corners as the theme fabric to determine the colors and fabrics for the entire quilt.

Grand Finale

Surface embroidery and hand quilting finish the quilt, adding that special touch of yesteryear.

GETTING STARTED

Strip size: 2¼"
Finished star size (tip to tip): approximately 38"
Finished quilt size: approximately 47" square
The layout is 4 x 4

Fabric Requirements

The fabrics in *Tea Time* are a collection of indigo blue and white floral designs, with yellow as the accent color. I encourage you to work with your collection of fabrics to create the teapots and central star. Blue and yellow fabrics are given as a guideline only.

FABRIC	AMOUNT	CUT
1 Lt. yellow	1¼ yard	1 - 2" strip (star center) 8 - 12" squares
2 Dk. navy blue	¼ yard	1 - 2" strip (star center) 1 - 1" strip (appliqué diamond)
3 Lt. yellow and blue print	¼ yard	2 - 2¼" strips
4 Blue floral prints, white background	¼ yard	3 - 2¼" strips
5 Med. blue prints	½ yard	4 - 2¼" strips (star center) 16 - fluted shapes (do not cut until directed)
6 Dk. blue print	¼ yard	2 - 2¼" strips
7 Med. tan with blue flowers	¼ yard	2 - 2¼" strips
8 Dk. blue print	⅛ yard	1 - 2¼" strips
9 Purchased valances OR antique tablecloth	At least 17 linear feet x 10" wide edging, whether lace or edges of tablecloth	do not cut until directed
10 Dk. blue print – outer "tablecloth" (appears beneath lace) and binding	2 yards	8 - trapezoids do not cut until directed
11 8 different pieces – teapots	scraps or fat eighths	1ea. - teapot
Assorted contrasting fabrics (small scale designs or solid)	scraps	accent pieces – lid, rim, spout, etc. for teapots; create as you prefer
Paper-backed fusible web	1 yard	8 - teapots accent pieces for teapots 16 - fluted shapes
Crocheted doilies (new or antiques)	4" round or square	8
100% cotton muslin (for blocking cloth)	½ yard	18" x 22" rectangle
Tear-away stablilizer	1 yard	

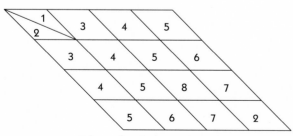

Enlarge for design paste-up.

Additional Tools & Equipment

Refer to page 50, and add the following:

Open toe embroidery foot

Appliqué pressing cloth

MAKING THE STAR

Special design features for this quilt are discussed here. Follow the basic Lone Star instructions in Chapter Four.

Split Diamonds

The center eight diamonds are created from two fabrics, split with a vertical seam. Construct them before assembling the strip sets.

1. Cut one strip 2" wide of each color fabric for the split diamonds.

2. Sew the two strips together, and press the seam open.

3. Mark the diamond size on the bottom of the 45° kaleidoscope ruler, as described on page 53. Turn the ruler over, and position the center guideline over the seam line.

4. Cut the first two sides of the diamond with a rotary cutter.

5. Rotate the ruler 180°, align the diamond outline with the cut edges, and cut the remaining two sides. Cut eight diamonds total.

Cutting split diamonds.

Note the arrangement of the split diamonds in the center of the quilt. To achieve the arrow design, alternate the diamond direction. To form a continuous pinwheel, alternate the colors light-dark-light-dark. The layout design you select determines how the individual split diamonds are sewn to the next fabric strip.

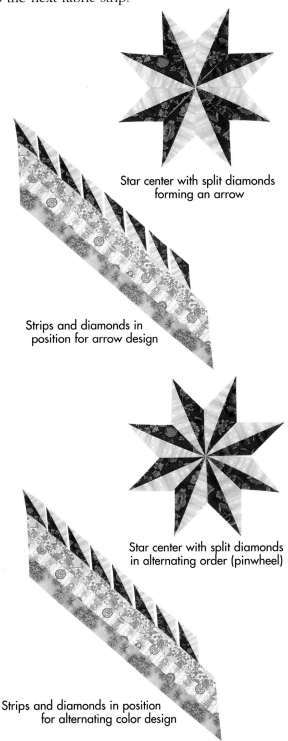

Star center with split diamonds forming an arrow

Strips and diamonds in position for arrow design

Star center with split diamonds in alternating order (pinwheel)

Strips and diamonds in position for alternating color design

Adding Split Diamonds to the Strips

1. Select the pre-cut split diamonds and the three fabrics for the first diamond row. Lay the strips in order, following the paste-up. Arrange the precut diamonds according to the center design you prefer. Allow ½" between individual diamonds for clean-up cuts.

2. Sew each diamond to the edge of an adjacent strip as shown on page 79. Make sure the strips match the original layout. Add strips 3 and 4, as usual.

3. Sew the remaining strip sets, for diamond rows 2, 3, and 4. Press all seams open.

4. Stack the strip sets while off-setting the upper edges, and cut eight stacks of diamond strips. Use the split diamond to position the ruler for each cut.

5. Assemble the eight diamond units for the central star. Block and press the seams open.

ADDING THE SETTING SQUARES

1. Measure the diamond units to determine the seam line, "X" (see page 58).

2. Draw a freezer paper pattern for the setting squares using "X" as the measurement. Add ¼" seam allowance on all sides of the square.

3. Position a 12" fabric square on top of the paper pattern.

4. With a pencil or water erasable pen, very lightly trace the paper square's finished dimension on the front of each fabric square. This outline helps when positioning the fluted shapes in the next step.

ADDING THE FLUTED APPLIQUÉ SHAPE

1. Cut two pieces of fusible web and two pieces of fabric 10" x 12". Trace eight fluted shapes on the paper side of one piece of web (pattern on page 109). Fuse the web to the back of each piece of fabric.

2. Place the marked and unmarked units fabric sides together. Holding the fabrics firmly together, roughly cut apart the traced shapes through all layers.

Fluted shape, teapot, and doily in position for stitching.

3. Keeping the two fabrics together, cut the traced shape with scissors and trim the straight edges with the rotary cutter. You have just created a mirror-image pair of fluted shapes. Repeat for all fluted shape pairs (total: sixteen fluted shapes, eight left and eight right).

4. Position and fuse the cut shapes on the setting squares with the raw edges aligned on two adjacent sides. The shapes should be about 1"-1½" from the corner. Set aside.

Making the Teapots

You can make the pots from a single fabric or combine different fabrics for spouts, handles, lids, and pot.

Tea Time teapot

1. Trace a master pattern for the teapot onto paper. Do not cut apart. Trace each teapot four times (patterns on page 109) on the paper side of the fusible web. The pattern is the reverse image of the finished pot. Roughly cut around the shape, allowing a margin for trimming later.

2. Trace and label all the teapot components: pot, rim, spout, lid, handle, and base. Trim away the inner area of web on the larger shapes only, leaving approximately ¼" of web inside the pen line.

Making a Teapot Using One Fabric

1. Position the fusible side of the trimmed shape to the wrong side of the fabric. Fuse following manufacturer's instructions.

2. Cut all eight pots on the outline. Set aside.

Teapot from one piece of fabric

Making a Teapot Using Several Fabrics

1. Prepare all components with fusible backing as described above. Trim to correct size. Place the master pattern for the teapot face up on the ironing board. Lay the appliqué pressing sheet or baking parchment over the pattern. (The pattern should be visible through the sheet.) Peel away the paper backing from all pieces for one pot.

2. Working in layers from back to front, build the image following the pattern. When satisfied with the design, press to adhere layers together. Allow teapot to cool and remove from the pressing sheet.

Finishing the Setting Squares

Using eight setting squares, doilies, and teapots, position the doilies on the plain lower corner, inside the seam allowance opposite the fluted appliqué shape corner. Audition teapot and doily combinations.

1. Place the square freezer paper pattern on the setting square, centering the motifs, making sure the straight edges of the fluted shapes align with the outer edge.

2. Pin or glue-baste doilies to the background squares. Topstitch the doilies by hand or machine as desired. Position, fuse, and topstitch the teapots in place.

3. Press each block thoroughly. The background fabric may have shrunk slightly during the appliqué process.

4. Trim the squares to the correct size including ¼" seam allowance.

5. Sew the setting squares to the diamonds as shown on page 59.

Creating the "Tablecloth" Borders

The trapezoid borders display a double layer of fabric, simulating a simple tablecloth and a decorative overskirt. You may use a variety of fabrics for either piece. Each selection will require slightly different methods to finish them. This is another design area where you have creative freedom!

Create your own embroidered tablecloth

Use a purchased tablecloth or valance over printed fabric for the double tablecloth.

Interesting Options for Overskirt Fabrics

Support fragile or worn fabrics, such as family linens or other antiques, with a lining or light-weight interfacing. Usually the outer edges are already hemmed and the corners can be used as they are.

A purchased valance also makes a good over-skirt due to its narrow width. Since they are already hemmed, you need only to miter the corners.

You may also design a stencil or embroidery pattern for the "tablecloth." Create patterns that complement the star center and teapot motifs. Consider using a narrow rolled hem, machine hem, or lining the fabric by sewing two layers right sides together, clipping the seam allowance, and turning the entire piece for a finished edge. Adding piping or lace around the outer edges for a finished appearance is another option.

Adding the Trapezoid Borders

1. Draw the trapezoid shape on freezer paper using the measurement of "X" for the side and top measurements. Add ¼" seam allowances to the top and sides. Add 1" to the bottom (longest) edge (refer to page 59 for full instructions).

2. Determine the top to bottom measurement for the overskirt by laying it on top of the base trapezoid and adjusting the two layers to your satisfaction.

3. Make a second template for the overskirt. The upper edge of both layers will be identical.

4. Cut eight trapezoids from the underskirt fabric, and cut eight overskirt units from your lace or linens.

5. Stitch the corner units, mitering the seams on both layers individually, creating an L shape. Leave inner seam allowances free, backstitching at the ¼" seam. Press seams open.

6. Layer the overskirt and fabric underskirt. Pin the raw edges together. Machine baste the upper edges with a ⅛" seam.

7. Add the completed trapezoid pieces to the body of the quilt following the Y-seam construction method in Chapter Four.

ADDING THE FINISHING TOUCHES

Baste and hand or machine quilt. Quilting through all layers of the "tablecloth" secures and finishes the design.

Tea Time quilt layout

Remembrance

✦ jan krentz

2000. 51" x 51"

BEHIND THE SCENES

Remembrance combines the traditional graphic appeal of a Lone Star with intricate pieced feather triangles. These elements distinguish Feathered Lone Star quilts from their simpler counterparts. This design is ideal for combining favorite quilt fabrics with a larger-scale home decorator fabric shown here. The decorator fabric is the focal point of this quilt. *Remembrance* features the Quilt for a Cure™ Botanical Collection by Timeless Treasures. Bright or dark accent fabrics were used sparingly for sparkle. Use fabrics currently available for your quilt.

Center Stage

The star's center features split diamonds in a 5 x 5 layout with color forming concentric rings from the center out to the tips. The fussy-cut double diamond units create a strong secondary pattern and feature the prominent medium- to large-scale print.

Supporting Cast

Surrounding the center star are fussy-cut setting squares that feature the flowers in the theme fabric.

In the Wings

A secondary row of pieced diamond units creates a wreath or halo surrounding the central star medallion. These are sewn from 2" strips, without the double diamond, and constructed at the same time that the central diamond units are cut and sewn. They are blocked to the same dimensions.

The size of the feathered corners is scaled to complement the center, repeating the general style and design of the quilt. The corner triangle is pieced in three sections to feature the printed cabbage roses and their leaves. Large-scale prints can be cut in different ways to utilize their beauty.

Star center

Grand Finale

Remembrance was machine quilted with feathered wreaths and curling tendrils in contrasting thread. Hidden among the nosegays are quilted butterflies.

GETTING STARTED

Strip size: 2"
Finished star size (tip to tip): approximately 36¼"
Finished quilt size: approximately 51" x 51"
The layout is 5 x 5

Fabric Requirements

Select readily available fabrics rather than search for out-of-date yardage. Showcase your favorite fabrics and colors, using a decorator or other large-scale print as the basis for your design.

This Feathered Lone Star features three areas with designer diamonds where the diamond is pre-pieced, fussy-cut, or unique in some way. The split diamonds on the sides create a sawtooth or feathered appearance to the edge of the star.

FABRIC	AMOUNT	CUT
1 Dk. burgundy	½ yard	4 - 2" strips 1 - 3½" strip
2 Med. rose print	½ yard	4 - 2" strips 1 - 3½" strip
3 Med. pink & green print	½ yard	5 - 2" strips
4 Med. blue-green print	⅓ yard	4 - 2" strips
5A Theme print – large scale printed fabric, light background	4-5 yards (necessary to fussy-cut setting squares, double diamonds and corner triangle sections)	do not cut until directed
5B Companion print, same background as theme fabric, above	¾ yard	5 - 3½" strips
6 Lt. tan print	¼ yard	2 - 2" strips
7 Med. tan print	⅝ yard	6 - 2" strips 1 - 3½" strip
8 Med.-dk. Forest green	⅓ yard	3 - 2" strips 1 - 3½" strip
9 Med. blue	⅝ yard	6 - 2" strips 1 - 3½" strip
10 Lt. pink print	⅓ yard	4 - 2" strips
100% cotton muslin (for blocking cloth)	½ yard	11" x 22" rectangle

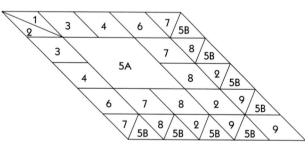

5 x 5 diamond layout for Feathered Star
Enlarge for paste-up

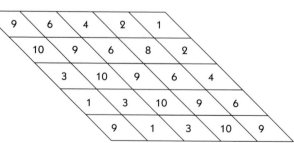

Paste-up for secondary diamond
Enlarge for paste-up

NOTE: To accommodate the different designer diamonds you will have sets of strips in varying numbers.

MAKING THE STAR

1. Complete your design paste-up as described on page 51.

2. Make a 3½" x 3½" double diamond template and fussy-cut eight double diamonds from the theme fabric.

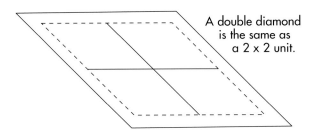

A double diamond is the same as a 2 x 2 unit.

Making the Split Diamonds

1. The star's eight center diamonds are created from two fabrics, split with a vertical seam. Construct them before assembling the strip sets (see page 79).

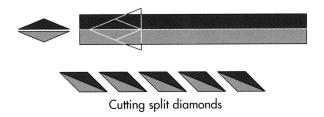

Cutting split diamonds

2. Sew the 3½" strips together, alternating star colors with background colors (5B-6-5B-7-5B-1-5B-8-5B). Press all seams open.

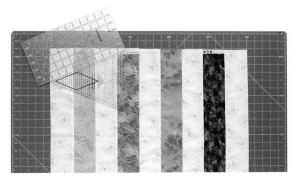

Pieced strips, alternating colors for Feathered Star

3. Mark the underside of the kaleidoscope ruler with the 2" diamond. Draw a line crosswise through the diamond from side to side. Align the center guideline with a pieced seam, and place a 12" or 24" acrylic ruler snugly beside the kaleidoscope ruler. Remove the kaleidoscope ruler and make the first angled cut across the entire strip set. Begin cutting 2" strips, checking the angle from time to time, making a fresh clean-up cut as necessary for accuracy.

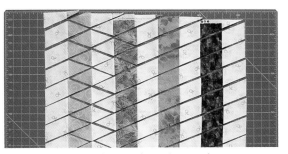

4. Align the horizontal line with the pieced seam, cutting sixteen split diamonds from each color combination.

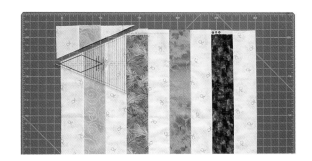

First cut of feathered diamonds

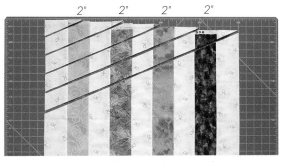

Second cut to form diamonds

Making the Strip Sets

1. Select the eight vertically split diamonds and the three fabrics for the first strip set.

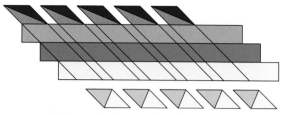

Adding split diamonds to the strip set.

2. Lay the three strips in order, following the paste-up, and sew them together.

3. Arrange the eight center diamonds across the top of the strip set. Allow ½" between individual diamonds for clean-up cuts. Sew the diamonds to the strip set. Cut eight strips at a 45° angle. Sew the corresponding "feather" (horizontally split diamond) to the bottom of each strip set.

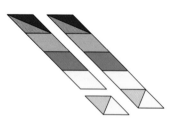

4. Select the 2" strips for the remaining solid diamonds in the center diamond unit. Lay strips in assembly order using the paste-up as a guide.

5. Sew together the two strips at the top of the double diamond. Press seams open. Turn the set face down for stack cutting, since these need to be angled the opposite direction from the other diamonds.

6. Choose the two strips and feather diamond for the two diamond units under the double diamond. Sew one group of feather diamonds to each strip. Press seams open.

7. Cut the strip set using the feathered diamonds to determine the 45° angle.

8. Sew the two diamond pairs together creating a 2 x 2 unit. Press seams open.

9. For the fourth row, select four strips of fabric and sew the strip set. Add a single row of feathered diamonds to the bottom of the set and sew. Press seam open. Cut eight, using the feathered diamond for the 45° cut.

10. For the 5th row cut eight single diamonds of fabric 9. Assemble the row according to your paste-up.

11. Lay out the diamond unit. Position the individual sections while checking for the correct angle and comparing with the master paste-up. Correct any errors that may have occurred.

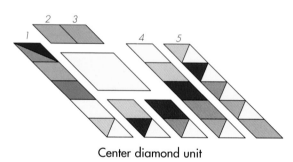

Center diamond unit

12. Sew the sub-units together according to the paste-up.

13. Measure interior diamonds and create a blocking cloth. Block and press seams open. Measure diamond units for "X" (approx. 10⅝"; be sure to use your measurement), and set units aside.

ADDING SETTING SQUARES, CORNERS, AND BORDERS

1. Draw a setting square template on freezer paper. Add ¼" seam allowance to all sides.

2. Fussy-cut the squares from your theme fabric.

3. Sew the setting squares using Y-seam construction as shown in Chapter Four.

Setting squares

4. Make the secondary diamond units according to the basic instructions in Chapter Four, carefully following your paste-up. Block on the blocking cloth. Press seams open.

5. Following the instructions in Chapter Four, construct the center star and add the setting square.

Secondary diamonds

6. Sew the secondary diamonds to the setting squares using Y-seam construction on page 62.

Creating the Feathered Corners

Corners feature the theme flowers

1. To draw the corner unit, use an 18" square piece of freezer paper and cut it diagonally to create two triangles. Draw a line measuring "2X" forming the longest side of the triangle. This side of the triangle fits against two diamond units.

2. Draw sides 2 and 3 at 45° angles to create a right triangle. This 90° intersection will be the outer corner of the quilt.

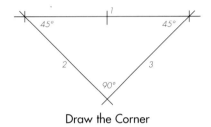

Draw the Corner

3. Draw parallel lines along the triangle's two short sides the same width (1¾") as the last row of diamonds in the adjacent unit.

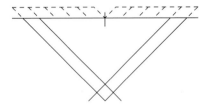

This forms the outside border

4. Divide both rows evenly into five sections with diagonal lines, creating triangles, as shown. (These will not be true 45° diamonds or half-square triangle units.)

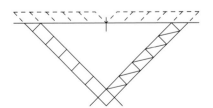

Dividing the edge border into five equal sections. Adding diagonal lines creates triangles.

5. To divide the center triangle into thirds. Use the center point and draw two lines at 60° angles to the outer edge as illustrated. This is your master pattern. Do NOT CUT APART.

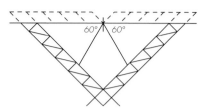

Master pattern for feathered corner

6. Stack four sheets of paper under this pattern and staple the corners; remove the thread from your sewing machine and sew through all the lines.

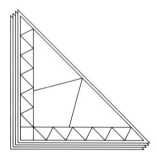

Mass producing foundation patterns

7. Remove the master pattern and label all sections of each corner triangle for fabric placement.

8. Cut one row of feathers from the main triangle with the outermost square attached as shown.

9. Cut the remaining row of feathers from the other side of the triangle.

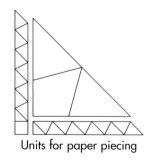

Units for paper piecing

10. Paper-piece the feather strips beginning at the square. Use a short (1.5mm) stitch for ease of tearing away the paper. Leave ¼" seam allowance beyond the paper on all sides when trimming the outer edge of the feather strip.

11. Cut the large triangle into three sections. Press each pattern piece to the wrong side of the theme fabric selectively centering the fabric motifs. Trim, leaving a ¼" seam allowance on all sides.

12. Construct the large triangle with these three pieces. Press. Sew the feathered strips to the large triangle. Carefully remove paper and press.

13. Sew the corner units to the quilt top. Press all seams.

ADDING THE FINISHING TOUCHES

Quilt by hand or machine as you prefer.

Remembrance quilting by Lisa Taylor

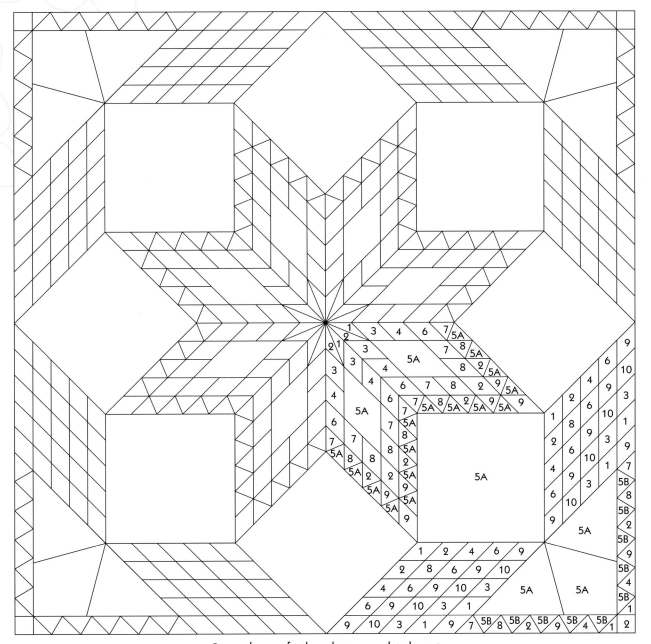

Remembrance feathered star complete layout

Spiral Lone Star

✶ jan krentz

2000. 46" x 46"

BEHIND THE SCENES

Visually dynamic, this graphic show-stopper is easier than expected to construct. Like the other stars, this one is strip pieced. The setting squares and corners are paper pieced. Secondary diamond units are strip pieced with special seam inserts that add sparkle.

Center Stage

A special cutting and piecing order creates the subtle color spiral. Equal amounts of each fabric are cut. The piecing sequence creates the spiral effect.

Supporting Cast

Quarter-compasses are foundation pieced on freezer paper to ensure accuracy. Metallic lamé fabrics, satins, and ribbons add visual pizzazz.

In the Wings

The large outer diamond units continue the spiral movement of color. They are easy to piece without distortion.

Compass square

Grand Finale

Paper-pieced compass corners finish the design.

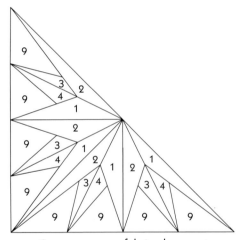

Compass corner fabric placement

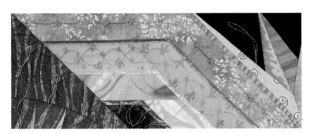

Outer diamond units with narrow accent strips

¼ spiral to use for design ideas.
Enlarge 200%

Compass corner

GETTING STARTED

Strip size: 2¼"

Finished star size (tip to tip): approximately 33½"

Finished quilt size: approximately 46" x 46"

Layout is 4x4

Fabric Requirements

You need sufficient contrast between the fabrics to easily see the spiral effect.

Color Chart

The color order is most important. Create a color chart by placing the fabrics in light to dark order, numbered one through eight. Select an additional fabric (number nine) for the outside background. This Spiral Lone Star has a black background in the corners. Select contrasting colors for the compass points to stand out against the background fabric. Study the numbered designs on page 98, and understand the placement of each color from row to row before beginning assembly.

COLOR	YOUR FABRIC SWATCHES
1	
2	
3	
4	
5	
6	
7	
8	
9	

NOTE: due to unraveling and heat sensitivity, specialty fabrics are recommended for intermediate to advanced quilters only. Skilled beginners should work with cotton fabrics.

FABRIC	AMOUNT	CUT
1 Yellow	¾ yard	All fabrics will be cut in the same amounts. Stack and cut, according to instructions below.
2 Yellow - orange	¾ yard	
3 Orange - peach	¾ yard	
4 Orange - red	¾ yard	5 - 2¼" strips
5 Red - violet	¾ yard	1 - 11" square
6 Violet	¾ yard	Use remaining yardage for paper piecing in compass blocks and compass corner.
7 Blue - violet	¾ yard	
8 Blue - black	¾ yard	
9 Black (background in compass corners)	½ yard	Do not cut until directed
Optional specialty fabrics: lamé shiny brocade (light weight), etc – several pieces in several colors to accent fabrics above	¼ to ½ yard	1 or 2 - 1" strips for folded inserts 1 or 2 - strips to use for paper piecing
Fusible interfacing (light weight) – to stabilize specialty fabrics	1 yard	Cut as needed to fuse to back of specialty fabrics
100% cotton muslin (for blocking cloth)	½ yard	1 - 11" x 22"

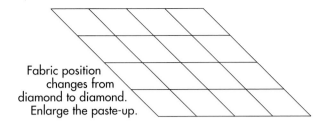

Fabric position changes from diamond to diamond. Enlarge the paste-up.

MAKING THE STAR

This is fun! Wait until you see the clever way the colors piece together and the pattern appears! First, create the central and secondary diamond units. Next, foundation-piece the compass setting squares and corners. You will assemble all the components of each unit before assembling the quilt top.

1. Lay out four strip set combinations:

1 - 2 - 3 - 4
3 - 4 - 5 - 6
5 - 6 - 7 - 8
7 - 8 - 1 - 2

Stagger and sew the first two strips of each group with a partial seam (about 15"). Sew the remaining strips in each group, creating all four strip sets. Press seams open.

2. Make a clean-up cut. Cut four 2¼" rows of diamonds from each strip set. Label with the top strip number (1 - 3 - 5 - 7).

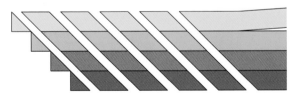

Strips 1-2-3-4, sewn and cut into 4 diamond rows.

3. Remove the partially sewn top strips. Re-arrange them, sewing a partial strip to the bottom edge of each strip set, creating the following combinations:

2 - 3 - 4 + 5
4 - 5 - 6 + 7
6 - 7 - 8 + 1
8 - 1 - 2 + 3

Center stage

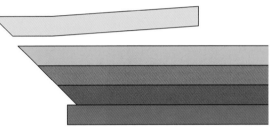

Remove strip 1 (top). Add strip 5 (bottom).

4. Press the seams open. make a clean-up cut. Cut four 2¼" rows of diamonds from each strip set. Label with the top strip number (2 - 4 - 6 - 8).

Assembled strips 2-3-4-5.
Cut four diamond strips from this group.

Eight diamond strip combinations

5. Lay out the spiral star on your design wall following the numbered diagram. The spiral pattern appears dramatically as you place strip sets into position.

6. Sew the diamond units; measure the finished diamonds for "X", and create a blocking cloth (refer to page 56). Block all eight diamond units. Mark the ¼" seam at all corners.

PIECING THE SECONDARY DIAMOND UNITS

The secondary diamond units are pieced from straight strip sections, cut in half using a template and sewn with a center seam.

1. To create a template, place template plastic over the blocking cloth (from step 6 above). With a permanent pen, trace one 45° tip. With the ruler, draw a line across the center of the diamond. Add ¼" seam allowance to that center line only. Cut the template on the lines.

2. Following the color numbering guide on page 99, select one 2¼" strip of each color. Prepare 2¼" strips with optional accent colors (see tip box). Sew strips together in the following combinations: 1 - 2 - 3 - 4; 3 - 4 - 5 - 6; 5 - 6 - 7 - 8; 7 - 8 - 1 - 2

Strips are sewn with selvages aligned using a scant ¼" seam. Press.

3. Fold the strip sets in half with right sides together. Position the template near the selvage end, aligning one long edge with the bottom strip as shown. Cut through both layers creating two mirror image pieces. The color sequence is continued from the central star, following the same progression from 1 through 8. Be consistent, keeping the strips laid out in order, and cutting each strip set in the same manner.

technique toolbox!

INSERT A SLIVER OF COLOR IN THE SEAM LINE

Insert narrow bands of color in the seams; select one accent color or specialty fabric to enhance each of the 8 fabrics.

 * Cut 1" strips from each accent fabric.
 * Pin the 1" accent fabric strip to the right side of the corresponding 2¼" fabric strip, aligning raw edges.
 * Using your machine's ½" seam guide, stitch the 2 fabrics together. Fold the accent strip in half, aligning all raw edges. Press with a cool iron.
 * Lay strips in the correct sequence, with accent strips consistently at the bottom. Sew the star strips together with SCANT ¼" seams.

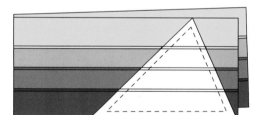

Cut carefully to get two sets from one strip set.

You will have two halves of a diamond from each strip set above; the last color number is the longest piece in the segment. Set these pairs aside.

4. Remove the top strip from each strip set. Rearrange and add the partial strip, to create the following four strip sets, which complete the color sequence: 2 - 3 - 4 + 5; 4 - 5 - 6 + 7; 6 - 7 - 8 + 1; 8 - 1 - 2 + 3.

5. Using the templates, cut the remaining four pairs of half-diamonds, for eight pairs total.

6. Sew the half units together along the short side, matching seams. Using the blocking cloth, press the center seam open. You now have eight secondary diamond units. Mark the ¼" seam allowance and set aside.

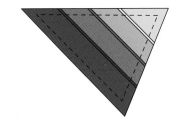

One half secondary diamond unit

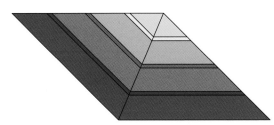

Complete secondary diamond unit

CREATING THE SETTING SQUARES
Paper-pieced Quarter-Compass Setting Squares

1. Draw the setting squares as described on page 58 in Chapter Four, using your "X" measurement.

2. Cut eight pieces of freezer paper large enough to trace the compass patterns. Using the compass pattern on page 107, trace one complete setting square compass. Staple and mass-produce eight squares (as described on page 90). Remove staples and separate. Color-code and number the compass patterns for assembly.

3. Cut away the curved background and center sections from each square. Set aside.

4. Separate the compass wedges into sections as shown. Do not cut all pieces apart.

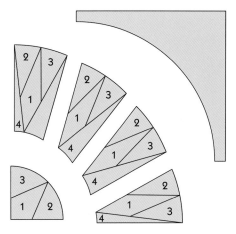

Separate background, fan, and center sections
Numbers indicate assembly order

5. Press one freezer paper background arc to the wrong side of each of the 11" fabric squares. Add ¼" seam allowance to the inside curve and cut.

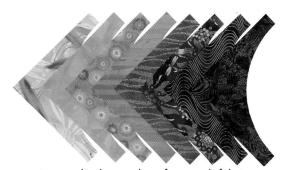

Cut one background arc from each fabric.

6. Set the machine to 12–15 (1.5mm-2mm) stitches per inch. Paper piece the compass sections, using the remaining fabrics for the background wedges, and scraps or narrower fabric strips for the slender compass rays. Optional: Add visual pizzazz to the slender rays by including metallic lamé, foiled fabrics, satins, and ribbons in matching colors in the fabric palette. Remember to trim and allow ¼" seam allowance on each section.

7. Sew the compass sections together, pinning to align sections. Press all seams.

8. Construct the eight small quarter-circles. Trim, allowing ¼" seam allowance on all sides. Sew the compass arcs to the background sections, and add the small quarter-circles. Block to size.

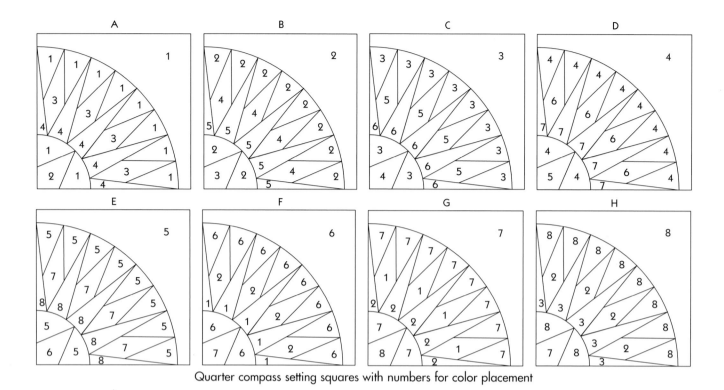

Quarter compass setting squares with numbers for color placement

MAKING THE CORNER COMPASSES

1. Draw a corner triangle on freezer paper using 2X as the longest side. Trace the compass pattern inside the triangle (2 sections directly from the pattern and 2 reversed). Draw 4 corners. Label the sections with the fabric colors above and piecing order, see page 97.

2. Paper piece these units using background fabric between the points, leaving ¼" seam allowances when trimming. Make four complete corners. Press.

3. Assemble the Spiral Star following the diagrams on page 99 using Y-seam construction. Remove foundation paper from the setting squares before basting the quilt.

ADDING THE FINISHING TOUCHES

Baste the quilt top with batting and backing. Quilt by hand or machine as you prefer. My quilt is free-motion quilted with a peacock head and feathers in the central star medallion. The setting squares, secondary diamond units, and compass corners have free-motion squiggles and knot shapes.

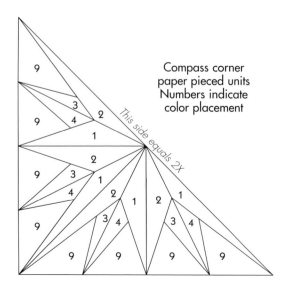

Compass corner
paper pieced units
Numbers indicate
color placement

This side equals 2X

Spiral Lone Star corner detail

Spiral Lone Star quilt layout

Summer Salsa

✷ jan krentz

1998. 46" x 46"

BEHIND THE SCENES

Summer Salsa features warm tones of red-orange, gold, lime green, teal, purple, and black. *Double Cappuccino*, on page 44, is the same pattern with entirely different colors. Select your favorite collection of fabrics, and create a totally new theme for your quilt. Remember to include dark, medium, and light values and a contrasting color for balance. The fabric colors specified here are for the *Summer Salsa* color layout. Generous yardage is suggested to allow for cutting, shrinkage, and other variables.

Center Stage

The fussy-cut center diamonds feature stripes that radiate from the center, creating a dramatic focal point. This 4 x 4 layout is simple to construct; the choice of fabrics makes the star look more complex than it is.

In the Wings

The eight setting squares are "rocket" blocks that are assembled using simple piecing methods—either with templates or paper-piecing. Once the blocks are sewn, experimenting with their orientation by turning them in different directions reveals interesting secondary patterns that support the center star.

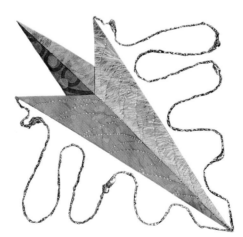

Star center

Supporting Cast

The secondary pieced diamond units are cut and sewn at the same time as the center star units. Note that the color bands run from tip to tip, creating a secondary ring or halo surrounding the center star. The four outer corners are half Mariner's Compasses. Like the rockets in the setting squares, the corners are pieced using freezer paper templates.

Grand Finale

Salsa is covered with a combination of machine quilting in the center, couched slubby yarns in the setting squares, beading throughout, and couching in the outer compass points. Creative continuous patterns are attractive and fun to stitch.

GETTING STARTED

Strip size: 2¼"
Finished star size (tip to tip): approximately 33½"
Finished quilt size: approximately 46" x 46"
The layout is 4x4

Fabric Requirements

Ample yardage is given allowing for artist's design changes.

Make the paste-up design sheet, including the rocket blocks and outer corners. Enlarge them for ease of working.

FABRIC	AMOUNT	CUT
1 Black – solid (background)	1 to 1½ yards	Rocket background: compass corner background) do not cut until you assemble the blocks
2 Black with colored stripe or print	¼ yard	1 - 2¼" strip OR 8 - fussy-cut diamonds
3 Bold, med./dk. batik or print	¾ yard	6 - 2¼" strips
4 Lime – bright	¼ yard	Used in rocket block
5 Lime – medium	¾ yard	6 - 2¼" strips compass corners
6 Lime – med./dk.	¼ yard	1 - 2¼" strip
7 Gold – med.	¼ yard	Used in rocket blocks/ compass corners
8 Orange – bright (accent)	¼ yard	1 - 2¼" strip
9 Orange – med.	½ yard	3 - 2¼" strips rocket blocks/compass corner
10 Rusty red-orange – med.	½ yard	2 - 2¼" strips rocket blocks/compass corners
11 Rusty red/orange – dk.	¼ yard	Used in rocket blocks/ compass corners
12 Teal (blue-green) – med.	¾ yard	4 - 2¼" strips rocket blocks/compass corners
13 Blue – dk.	¾ yard	6 - 2¼" strips
14 Purple – dk.	½ yard	2 - 2¼" strips compas corners
Freezer paper		
100% cotton muslin (blocking cloth)	½ yard	1 - 11" x 22"

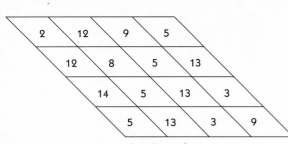

Center Diamond. Enlarge for paste-up.

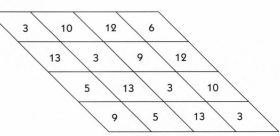

Secondary Diamond. Enlarge for paste-up.

MAKING THE STAR

1. Strip piece all diamond units. Sew eight center diamonds and eight secondary diamonds.

2. Make the blocking cloth and block the diamond units. Measure for "X" (it will be approximately 9¾" but be sure to use your "X" measurement).

Making Rocket Block Setting Squares

Each rocket block requires a paper piecing foundation.

1. Enlarge the rocket block pattern on page 108 by 139%, the outside measurement should be approximately 9¾". If your "X" measurement is slightly different use your "X" measurement.

2. Trace the rocket block on one square of freezer paper. Mass-produce 8 paper foundations as described on page 90.

3. Number the pattern pieces for color placement and piecing order. Cut the paper foundation on the diagonal line, creating 2 halves.

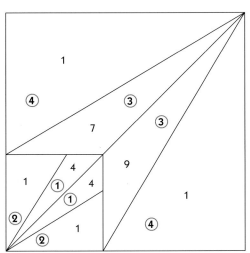

Rocket block pattern. Circled numbers in BOLD print indicate the piecing order.

Rocket block

4. Paper piece the block, following the piecing order indicated on the illustration. Trim, allowing ¼" on all sides.

5. Sew the center seam. Carefully remove the freezer paper. Repeat to construct the eight rocket blocks.

6. Press, then mark the ¼" intersections on all four corners of each block as you did for the diamond units.

Making the Compass Corners

Each compass corner requires four patterns (2 reversed).

1. The compass corner pattern on page 107 is full size, the longest side should be 9¾". If your "X" measurement is slightly different use your "X" measurement. Add ¼" seam allowances on all sides.

2. Trace the compass corner pattern on page 107 onto the freezer paper triangles four times for each corner. Number all pattern pieces. Cut the pattern apart keeping the pieces for each individual corner unit together—do not mix pieces from different corners, as they may not be cut identically.

3. Use pre-cut fabric strips to work the narrow compass rays, and pre-cut oversized background shapes for the outer edges. Piece the sections on freezer paper and trim.

4. Using the freezer paper shapes as templates, remember to place two sets right side up and two reversed on your fabrics for each corner.

5. Adding ¼" seam allowances on all sides cut your fabrics. Construct the four compass corners, pinning carefully as you assemble the sections.

6. Press, then mark the ¼" intersections on all four corners of each block as you did for the center diamond and rocket blocks.

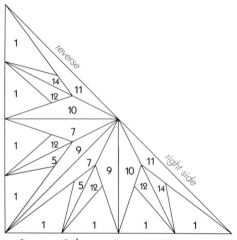

Summer Salsa compass corner paste-up

PUTTING IT ALL TOGETHER

1. Sew the center diamond units, rocket blocks, and secondary diamonds following the basic Y-seam construction in Chaper Four.

2. Sew the compass corners to the outer diamonds. Press.

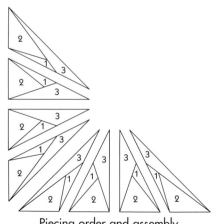

Piecing order and assembly

Summer Salsa beading.

ADD THE FINISHING TOUCHES

Baste the quilt top with batting and backing. Hand or machine quilt as you like. This quilt lends itself to embellishment with beading, couching, embroidery, or appliqué as you prefer. Refer to Chapter Six for embellishment suggestions.

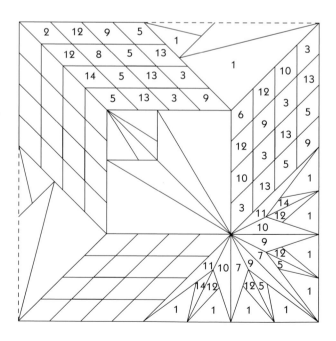

Summer Salsa quilt layout

Embellishment Techniques

EMBELLISHMENT SUPPLIES

* Decorative threads, cords, ribbons, laces
* Beads, baubles, trinkets, found items, shells, buttons, etc.
* Needles, beeswax, or silicone lubricant
* Teflon pressing sheet or baking parchment paper for fusing designs

Beading

Selecting beads to enhance a star quilt is an art akin to fabric selection or choosing a quilting design. Consider the same elements used in fabric selection: color, texture, contrast, size, and light reflectivity.

A quilt may require a significant number of beads to create an interesting visual effect. Sew beads to the quilt surface after the quilting is finished. Tie knots frequently while attaching beads to the surface, to prevent loss of beads in the event the thread should break. Using this method, missing beads can easily be replaced.

Couching and Embroidery

There are many excellent books available that discuss embroidery techniques in depth. Surface embellishment covers a wide variety of needlework, including couching and embroidery. Couching is a simple decorative process for adding texture to the quilt's surface, as seen on *Summer Salsa*. Dimensional threads are stitched to the quilt after quilting.

Couching by Hand

Couching is added after the quilting process is complete. Simply coil or squiggle the thread across the surface until you are satisfied with the position. Pin the cord in place, and stitch it by hand, securing the decorative thread as you stitch it to the quilt's surface. The ends may be threaded into a large-eye tapestry needle, and hidden between the quilt's layers, or wrapped tightly and stitched to the quilt's surface.

Couching by Machine

Select a smooth cord or yarn, use a couching foot (a special attachment), and a zigzag stitch sewing machine. Set the stitch width to fully cover the cord without piercing it. Draw a line on the quilt's surface, and slowly follow the path, zigzagging over the cord as you follow the line on the fabric. You may want to use decorative thread and stitches to create a lovely combination of pattern stitches and cord. The couching may be done before piecing sections together—making it easier to hide the ends of the cord—or when the quilt top is finished.

Attached Dimensional Ornaments

Surface embellishment has been popular in the past decade. If you are creating a quilt to be used on the bed, to be cuddled with while reading or watching television, keep embellishments to a minimum. On the other hand, wall quilts, art quilts, and quilted garments are all candidates for added surface embellishment.

Shisha mirrors, buttons, yo-yos, or brass charms are the perfect elements to finish your quilt design, adding interesting sparkle and detail. Attaching "found" items can also lead to creative treatments. Some of these might be counted thread work, cut-out fabric "collars" that are stitched to the surface, sea shells, pebbles, and other natural items secured beneath sheer layers of netting or tulle. You are only limited by your imagination.

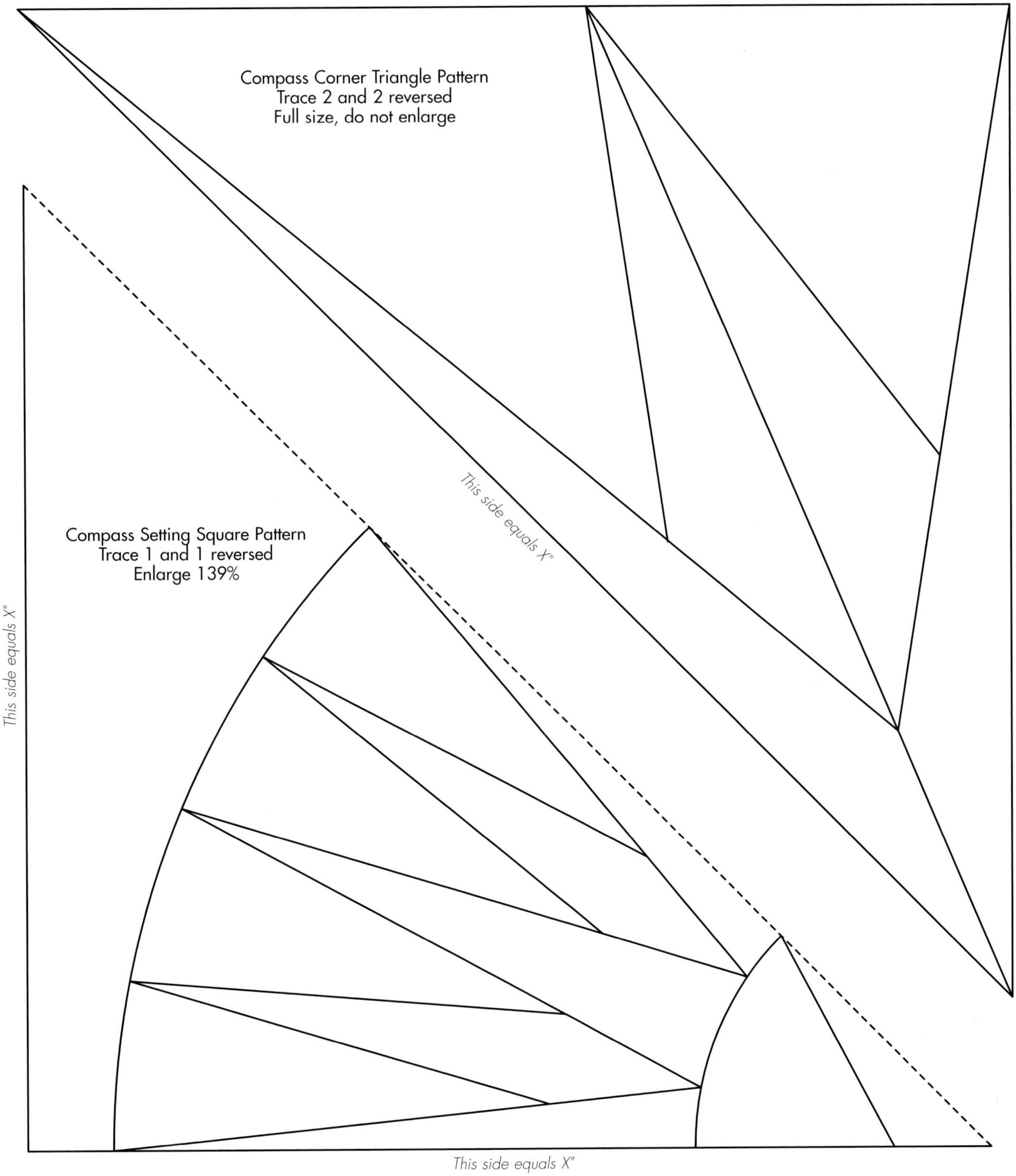

Compass Corner Triangle Pattern
Trace 2 and 2 reversed
Full size, do not enlarge

Compass Setting Square Pattern
Trace 1 and 1 reversed
Enlarge 139%

This side equals X"

This side equals X"

This side equals X"

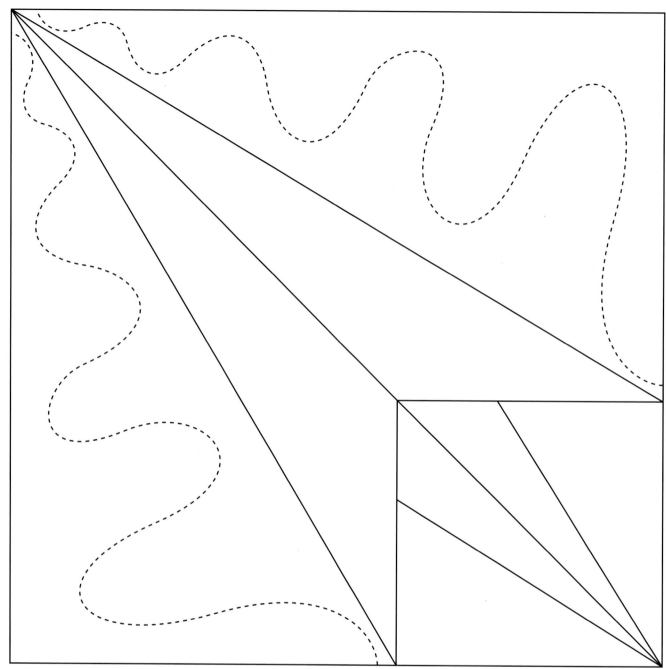

Rocket block pattern for *Summer Salsa*
Enlarge 139%

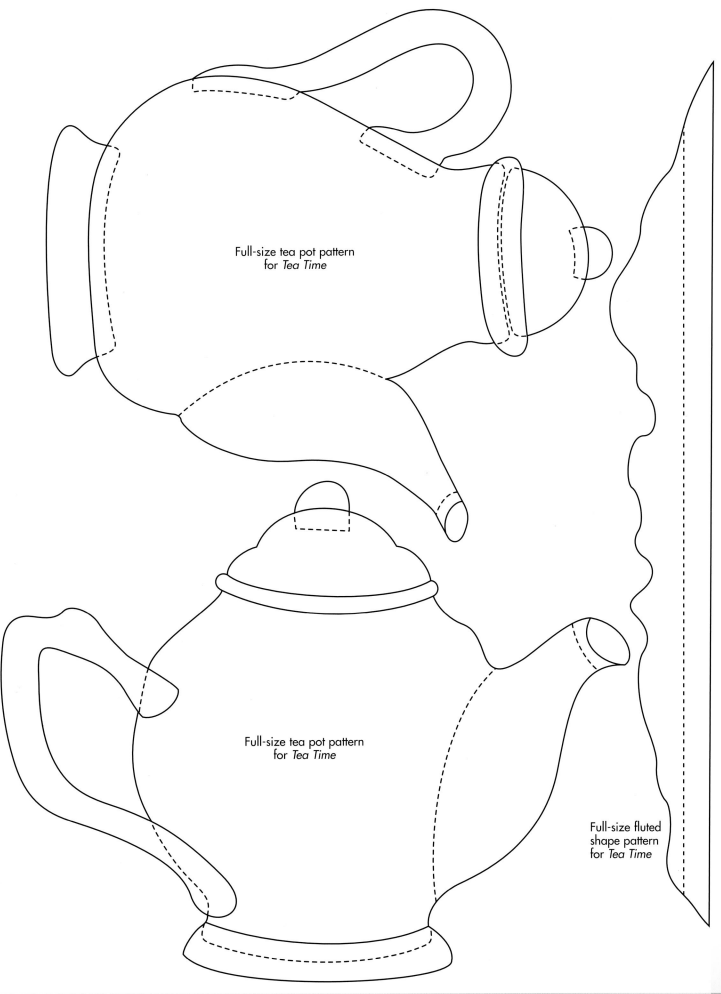

Full-size tea pot pattern
for *Tea Time*

Full-size tea pot pattern
for *Tea Time*

Full-size fluted
shape pattern
for *Tea Time*

FINISHED SIZES

The following chart provides an *approximate* guide to the finished dimension of a pieced star. Your star measurements may measure differently, due to the following variables:

✳ seam allowance (wider or narrow seam allowance will *significantly affect the finished size*)

✳ additional setting or layout pieces - the areas surrounding the star add dimension, changing the final measurement.

✳ additional borders - increase the final size and dimension of the quilt.

Star Layout = number of diamonds in a row

Diamond Size = both strip width and finished dimensions given

A = the finished seam length, measured from ¼" point to ¼" point (refer to measuring diamond units, page 58)

B = the horizontal / vertical measurement across the full width / height of the star

Diamond size strip width/finished size		3 x 3 Layout A	B	4 x 4 Layout A	B	5 x 5 Layout A	B	6 x 6 Layout A	B
2"	1½"	6⅜"	21¾"	8½"	29"	10⅝"	36¼"	12¾"	43½"
2¼"	1¾"	7⁵⁄₁₆"	25⅛"	9¾"	33½"	12³⁄₁₆"	41⅞"	14⅝"	50¼"
2½"	2"	8¼"	28½"	11"	38"	13¾"	47½"	16½"	57"
2¾"	2¼"	9⅜"	32¼"	12½"	43"	15⅝"	53¾"	18¾"	64½"
3"	2½"	10½"	36"	14"	48"	17½"	60"	21"	72"
3½"	3"	12⁹⁄₁₆"	43⅛"	16¾"	57½"	20¹⁵⁄₁₆"	71⅞"	25⅛"	86¼"
4"	3½"	14⅝"	50¼"	19½"	67"	24⅜"	83¾"	29¼"	100½"

Diamond size strip width/finished size		7 x 7 Layout A	B	8 x 8 Layout A	B	9 x 9 Layout A	B	10 x 10 Layout A	B
2"	1½"	14⅞"	50¾"	17"	58"	19⅛"	65¼"	21¼"	57½"
2¼"	1¾"	17¹⁄₁₆"	58⅝"	19½"	67"	21¹⁵⁄₁₆"	75⅜"	24⅜"	66¼"
2½"	2"	19¼"	66½"	22"	76"	24¾"	85½"	27½"	75"
2¾"	2¼"	21⅞"	75¼"	25"	94"	28⅛"	96¾"	31¼"	85"
3"	2½"								
3½"	3"								
4"	3½"								

INDEX

OTHER FINE BOOKS FROM C&T PUBLISHING:

250 Continuous-Line Quilting Designs for Hand, Machine & Long-Arm Quilters, Laura Lee Fritz

The Art of Machine Piecing: Quality Workmanship Through a Colorful Journey, Sally Collins

The Art of Classic Quiltmaking, Harriet Hargrave and Sharyn Craig

Block Magic: Over 50 Fun & Easy Blocks made from Squares and Rectangles, Nancy Johnson-Srebro

Cotton Candy Quilts: Using Feedsacks, Vintage and Reproduction Fabrics, Mary Mashuta

Crazy Quilt Handbook, 2nd Edition, Judith Montano

Cut-Loose Quilts: Stack, Slice, Switch & Sew, Jan Mullen

Do-It-Yourself Framed Quilts: Fast, Fun & Easy Projects, Gai Perry

Finishing the Figure: Doll Costuming • Embellishments • Accessories, Susanna Oroyan

Flower Pounding: Quilt Projects for All Ages, Amy Sandrin & Ann Frischkorn

Free Stuff for Home Repair on the Internet, Judy Heim and Gloria Hansen

Free Stuff for Pet Lovers on the Internet, Gloria Hansen

Free Stuff for Quilters on the Internet, 3rd Ed., Judy Heim and Gloria Hansen

Free Stuff for Traveling Quilters on the Internet, Gloria Hansen

Ghost Layers & Color Washes: Three Steps to Spectacular Quilts, Katie Pasquini Masopust

Great Lakes, Great Quilts: 12 Projects Celebrating Quilting Traditions, Marsha MacDowell

Hand Appliqué with Alex Anderson: Seven Projects for Hand Appliqué, Alex Anderson

In the Nursery: Creative Quilts and Designer Touches, Jennifer Sampou & Carolyn Schmitz

Laurel Burch Quilts: Kindred Creatures, Laurel Burch

Machine Embroidery and More: Ten Step-by-Step Projects Using Border Fabrics & Beads, Kristen Dibbs

Magical Four-Patch and Nine-Patch Quilts, Yvonne Porcella

Quilted Memories: Celebrations of Life, Mary Lou Weidman

Quilting Back to Front: Fun & Easy No-Mark Techniques, Larraine Scouler

Quilting with Carol Armstrong: 30 Quilting Patterns, Appliqué Designs, 16 Projects, Carol Armstrong

Shadow Redwork™ with Alex Anderson: 24 Designs to Mix and Match, Alex Anderson

Snowflakes & Quilts, Paula Nadelstern

Start Quilting with Alex Anderson, 2nd Edition: Six Projects for First-Time Quilters, Alex Anderson

Strips 'n Curves: A New Spin on Strip Piecing, Louisa Smith

Two-for-One Foundation Piecing: Reversible Quilts and More, Wendy Hill

For more information write for a free catalog:

C&T Publishing, Inc.
P.O. Box 1456
Lafayette, CA 94549
(800) 284-1114
e-mail: ctinfo@ctpub.com
website: www.ctpub.com

For quilting supplies:

Cotton Patch Mail Order
3405 Hall Lane, Dept. CTB
Lafayette, CA 94549
(800) 835-4418
(925) 283-7883
e-mail: quiltusa@yahoo.com
website: www.quiltusa.com

ABOUT THE AUTHOR

Jan Krentz is an active member of the quilting community. She is a teacher, designer, pattern maker, and author who inspires others to enjoy the art of quiltmaking. Jan started sewing at an early age, and is skilled in a variety of needlework disciplines.

Best known for her color selection and technical skill, Jan's quilts are beautifully distinctive. She began making quilts in 1973, and teaching the art of quiltmaking in 1982. She eagerly shares the art of quilting to all who will hear, and is a motivating teacher.

Jan was the recipient of the 1998 Teacher of the Year award, and has been featured in several national magazines. You can find Jan in *Quilting Workshops* (©2000), *Who's Who in American Quilting*, several of her quilts in Jean Ray Laury's *Photo Transfer Handbook* (©1999), and a feature article in *Traditional Quiltworks* magazine (July 1999).

You can contact Jan at the following address:
P.O. Box 722799
San Diego, CA 92172-2799

www.jankrentz.com